High School Chemistry

Archibald Patterson Knight

BIBLIOLIFE

HIGH SCHOOL CHEMISTRY.

BY

A. P. KNIGHT, M.A., M.D.,

Queen's University, Kingston,

AND

W. S. ELLIS, B.A., B.Sc.,

Collegiate Institute, Kingston.

Authorized by the Department of Education for Ontario.

TORONTO:

THE COPP, CLARK COMPANY, LIMITED.

PREFACE.

THIS book is intended to aid the teacher, not to supersede him. For this reason particular care has been taken to arrange the work in such a way that the student can learn only by doing the experiments under intelligent guidance. Except in rare cases the wording of an experiment or question gives no hint as to the result required.

Questions obviously arising out of the experiments, or such as a teacher would probably ask, for the purpose of developing his lesson, have been designedly omitted.

Under the heading "Additional Exercises" a considerable number of experiments have been inserted for the purpose of furnishing material (1) for a variety in the work from year to year, (2) to enable teachers to adapt their courses somewhat to the equipment of their schools, (3) to provide work for students who get along faster than the class, or who are going over their chemistry a second time.

It is assumed that students, before beginning chemistry, have a knowledge of elementary physics.

In an appendix will be found the syllabus of the Pass Matriculation course in chemistry for the next three years; also a list of books of reference suitable for this portion of high school work. The contents of this book are necessarily confined to the subjects there laid down, and it is intended that the work be done in one year.

KINGSTON, 1895.

CONTENTS.

———

APPENDIX.

EXPERIMENTAL CHEMISTRY

CHAPTER I.

The object of this chapter is to illustrate the various kinds of changes and apparent changes which matter may undergo.

1.—Physical Change.

EXPERIMENTS.

1. Heat a piece of platinum wire in the flame of a spirit lamp or gas burner.

2. Fill a test-tube full of water and invert it over a tumbler or beaker half-full of water, as in Fig. 1. Heat the upper end with a spirit lamp until steam forms, and then allow the test-tube to cool.

Fig. 1.

3. Hold a rod of hard glass in a gas flame until it becomes red hot, then pull the ends of the rod apart. After cooling can you observe any change in the properties of the glass at the place where it was heated?

2.—Chemical Change.

EXPERIMENTS.

1. Treat a piece of magnesium wire as you did the platinum of ex. 1, sect. 1.

2. Lay a bit of phosphorus about half as large as a pea on a piece of sheet zinc, set this on a plate, touch it with a hot wire, and then cover it with a bell jar.

3. Hold a splinter of wood or a piece of sealing wax in the gas flame until it takes fire.

3.—Questions and Exercises.

1. In sections 1 and 2, compare similarly numbered experiments and state what you observed in each case.

2. By comparison of experiments, as indicated in the last question, try to determine in what cases, only some of the properties of the substances acted on were changed, and in what cases entirely new substances were formed.

3. Mix a little sulphuric acid with twice its volume of water and divide the mixture into two parts, pouring each into a test-tube. Into one drop a piece of platinum wire, into the other a piece of magnesium wire, then hold a lighted match to the mouth of each tube. Is there a chemical change in either case? Upon what evidence is your answer based?

4. In sect. 1, the changes were **physical**, and in sect. 2, **chemical**; from this express in your own words what these consist of and what is the difference between them.

4.—Mixture and Combination.

EXPERIMENTS.

1. Prepare some fine iron filings (those formed when saws are sharpened answer well); to these add about

double their weight of powdered sulphur, and shake on a piece of paper until the two are thoroughly intermingled, then examine with a magnifying glass. Draw a magnet or a magnetized knife blade a number of times through the mixture. Divide the mixture into two parts, on one drop some hydrochloric acid and carefully smell the gas that comes off. Heat the other part in a test-tube or small crucible until it glows; after cooling, again examine it with glass and magnet, and then drop on it some hydrochloric acid and notice the odor of the gas formed.

2. Repeat this experiment but use copper filings instead of iron.

3. Mix some sand and common table salt (sodium chloride), both dry, after stirring them together examine with a magnifying glass. Pour water on the mixture, stirring it meantime, and when it has stood for a few minutes filter it; evaporate the **filtrate** (that which passes through the paper), also collect what remains on the paper and dry it.

4. Make a mixture of powdered sal ammoniac and charcoal, then heat over a water or sand bath for some time.

————

5.—Questions.

1. In ex. 1, sect. 4, were the iron and the sulphur distinguishable at any time after they were put together? Would your answer be applicable during the whole treatment which they received? What evidence is there that a new substance was formed?

A **mixture** (or mechanical mixture as it is sometimes called) is an intermingling of masses, even though very minute, of two or more substances, but each retains its own properties and identity.

6.—Solution.

EXPERIMENTS.

1. In a small beaker or test-tube place a little salt, then pour water on it until the vessel is nearly full; after standing awhile, taste the liquid by lifting a drop on the end of a piece of glass rod and placing it on the tongue.

2. Repeat this experiment using sugar instead of salt. Have the salt and sugar vanished?

3. Mix, in a test-tube, 1 part of sulphuric acid with 20 parts of water. Taste the mixture, and say whether the acid has dissolved in the water. Repeat this experiment using equal parts of alcohol and water.

4. Fit a test-tube with a good cork and delivery tube, as in Fig 2. Put in this tube about 2 cc. of spirits of hartshorn and invert a large dry test-tube over the mouth of the delivery tube; heat the hartshorn, and when the smell of ammonia is plainly discernible about the inverted tube, carefully place this tube, still inverted, with its mouth under water and let it stand there for a few minutes.

FIG. 2.

Explanation.—If there is a doubt as to whether a solid is soluble in a liquid, shake the two together, and after the solid particles settle to the bottom, lift out two or three drops of the clear liquid and *gently* evaporate this on a strip of clean glass, a bit of mica sheet, or a piece of platinum foil. If no trace of sediment is left the solid is insoluble, but if any sediment appears on the slip, it must have come from the clear fluid; hence some of the solid was dissolved in it.

When a substance disappears in a liquid, as in the case of salt or sugar in water, it is said to **dissolve**, the liquid

in which it disappears is called a **solvent,** and the resulting fluid a **solution.** The solution is **saturated** when
the liquid does not take up any more of the substance;
that is, when the liquid does not undergo any further
change in presence of the substance. A solution is
concentrated when it contains a relatively large portion of the dissolved substance, and it is **dilute** when
the liquid is present in considerable excess.

The solution of soluble substances is hastened by
(1) powdering the solid, (2) stirring it and the solvent
together, (3) suspending it in the liquid, (4) heating the
liquid. From the study of these methods it will readily
be seen that solution is entirely a surface operation.

7.—Questions and Exercises.

1. Fill a small test-tube to the depth of 4 c. with water, and then
add chloroform, or sulphuric ether, to the depth of 1 c. Shake well,
and allow the mixture to stand for a few minutes, after which,
examine it carefully.

2. Make a solution of iodine in iodide of potash solution; dilute
until the colour is a seal brown, then add a few drops of chloroform
and shake the two together. What does this show about the
relative solubility of iodine in water and in chloroform? Carefully
pour off the water, then turn the chloroform into an evaporating
dish and let it stand for half an hour. Does this experiment give you
any hint as to how iodine may be separated from water? Would
chloroform act in the same way on an alcoholic solution of iodine?

3. Pour about 2 cc. each of water, alcohol, sulphuric ether, chloroform, and carbon bisulphide into separate small test-tubes, then
into each let fall a couple of drops of oil and shake well. Can you
form any opinion as to the solubility of oil in these substances?

4. Where does a solid go to when dissolved?

5. How may a solid be obtained from a liquid in which it is dissolved?

6. Devise means of separating salt from sand, sugar from charcoal, iodine from iron filings; in each case saving both substances.

7. Perform the following operations and decide whether the change is a physical or chemical one in each case:—

(1) Heat, on a piece of mica, some white sugar until it blackens.

(2) Put some sugar in an evaporating dish and pour a little strong sulphuric acid on it, after standing for a few minutes, wash it well by turning a very light stream of water on it. Taste it.

(3) Hold the end of a strip of zinc in the gas flame until it melts.

(4) Take another piece of this zinc, put it in a test-tube and pour over it a little sulphuric acid diluted with twice its volume of water; after all bubbles cease to rise, evaporate the liquid.

8. How do you account for the bubbles of gas rising out of a bottle of soda water or of ginger ale when the stopper is removed? Pour a little soda water or ginger ale out of a newly-opened bottle into a test-tube and warm it.

9. Scatter some iron filings over a sheet of paper, then bring a magnet near the under side of the paper, and move it about beneath the filings. Is the change produced in the filings a physical or a chemical one?

8.—Additional Exercises.

1. Prepare some powdered nitrate of potash and some powdered charcoal, shake them together on a piece of paper, then divide into two parts, and heat one of these on a piece of mica. Compare the result with the other part of the substance that was on the paper. Have you a mixture, a compound, or both?

2. Take an ounce each of powdered alum, washing soda, and copper sulphate, and dissolve them separately in a fluid ounce of water each. Stir with a glass rod, and observe the extent to

which each one dissolves. Now heat the solutions until they boil, stir again, and notice whether there is any variation in solubility.

3. Carefully counterbalance on a scale a small beaker or dish containing a couple of grams of bicarbonate of soda, then add water little by little until the white solid disappears. Evaporate over a sand bath, or in a water bath, until the liquid all disappears. After thoroughly drying and cooling, compare the weight of the vessel and its contents with what it was at first.

4. Try, judging by the colour, if iodine is soluble in water, alcohol, solution of iodide of potash, ether, chloroform or bisulphide of carbon.

5. Try if nitrate of potash, red lead, bichloride of mercury (corrosive sublimate), sulphur and charcoal are soluble in water.

6. A blacksmith burns coal in his forge that he may make the iron hot and more easily worked ; how would you classify the changes in the coal and iron? Can you give any other examples of these changes from mechanical or domestic operations?

7. Gunpowder consists of charcoal, sulphur and nitre. Separate these substances in a given sample of gunpowder.

8. On some copper filings pour a little nitric acid, and gently warm; after the filings have disappeared, evaporate the substance left. Is the solid obtained soluble in water? How would you classify the action between the copper and the acid?

9. Tell how you would find out how much sand there is in 100 grams of the sugar of which your teacher will supply you with a sample. If the mixture had contained some copper filings also, how would you proceed?

10. How does the weight of a solution compare with the weights of the solid and liquid which form it?

11. Compare the density, color, taste and smell of a solution with the substances that enter into it.

CHAPTER II.

1.—Conditions that Promote Chemical Change.

In some cases substances will combine chemically if simply mixed, but generally it is necessary to resort to some special treatment in order to bring about chemical combination; similarly, compounds sometimes decompose spontaneously, but in most cases, the breaking up of a compound into its constituents results from methods adopted for that purpose.

The conditions that tend to promote chemical action are generally (1) either simply mixing, rubbing together, or dissolving the constituents, (2) exposing to higher temperature, (3) using electrical energy, (4) exposing to light, (5) using vital energy. Of these, solution and change of temperature are the ones more commonly employed.

2.—Intimate Mixture.

The production of chemical combination is often dependent on the bringing of the minute parts of the constituents into very near contact with each other. The methods adopted for accomplishing this result are generally (1) stirring the substances together, (2) rubbing or pounding them together, (3) mixing solutions of them.

EXPERIMENTS.

1. Wet the inside of a slightly warmed glass beaker with strong aqua ammoniæ, and the inside of another beaker with a strong solution of hydrochloric acid; cover

the first beaker with a glass plate and invert over the second.   Then draw out the plate.

2. Cut a thin slice from the end of a stick of phosphorus.*   Dry it well and place on a plate, then sprinkle over it a little powdered iodine.   Cover with a wide-mouthed bottle.

3. In a small dish or test-tube put a piece of freshly cut phosphorus and cover it with a strong solution of silver nitrate ; let it stand for 24 hours.

4. Powder a little chlorate of potash and dry it well on a warm glass or on mica, then mix with it half its own bulk of sulphur, by shaking them together on a piece of paper (they must not be stirred or rubbed). Place a *little* of the mixture on some hard object, such as a smooth stone or an iron plate ; either strike this mixture with a hammer or rub it with a large pestle. *This experiment is dangerous unless the directions are followed.*

5. Mix a teaspoonful of baking soda (sodium bi-carbonate, $NaHCO_3$) and half as much oxalic acid, $H_2C_2O_4$, in a large test-tube ; shake them well together, then pour in a little water.   Vary this experiment by mixing the two substances when dry; also dissolve portions of them separately and mix the solutions.

6. Dissolve a few crystals of iodide of potassium, KI, and of lead acetate, $Pb(C_2H_3O_2)_2$, in separate test-tubes, then mix the solutions.

---

*Always cut phosphorus under water, and always hold it with a pair of forceps —never in the fingers.

3.—Heat.

Substances when heated will often undergo chemical change, both of combination and decomposition, while at ordinary temperatures they are chemically inert.

EXPERIMENTS.

1 Place about half an inch in depth of chlorate of potash, $KClO_3$, in a test-tube and heat it strongly until it melts, and bubbles of gas begin to come off, then hold in the mouth of the tube a glowing splinter. After the heating has been continued for about five minutes, allow the tube and its contents to cool, then dissolve the solid residue. At the same time make a solution of some of the original chlorate; into each, drop a little silver nitrate solution.

2. Heat some red oxide of mercury, HgO, in a test-tube and hold a glowing splinter in the mouth of the tube.

3. Make a mixture of some powdered chlorate of potash and white sugar, put a little of this on a piece of mica and heat it. Vary the experiment by letting fall a drop or two of sulphuric acid from the end of a glass rod on a portion of the mixture.

4.—Light.

EXPERIMENTS.

1. Moisten a piece of paper with nitrate of silver solution, then lay on this paper a leaf of a plant, cover the whole with a piece of glass and expose to sunlight.

2. Repeat experiment 1, but use bichromate of potash solution instead of silver nitrate.

3. To some dilute solution of silver nitrate add some solution of common salt, allow the precipitate which will be formed to stand in sunlight for a time.

A **precipitate** (p'p'te.) is a solid substance formed in a liquid or a mixture of liquids, and is consequently insoluble in the fluid in which it is formed.

5.—Electricity.

1. Pass a current of electricity through water in a decomposition-of-water apparatus, as in Fig. 3. This will require a current from about 4 bichromate cells " in series." (See High School Physical Science).

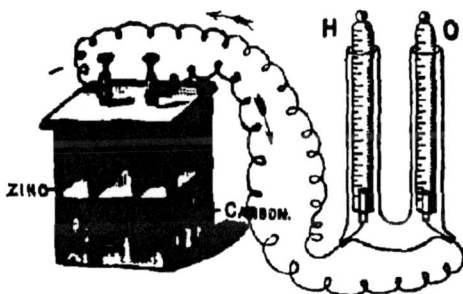

FIG. 3.

6.—Vital Force.

EXPERIMENT.

1. Make a weak solution of sugar in water and add to it a little yeast powder. Let this stand for a few days in a warm place. Taste the liquid.

7.—Questions and Exercises

1. Make a mixture of powdered sulphate of iron (copperas), $FeSO_4$, and ferrocyanide of potash (yellow prussiate of potash),

K_4FeCy_6. Drop some water on the mixture. What does this show?

2. A match may be lit by rubbing it against a rough surface, or by holding it against a hot object. Give reasons why.

3. By what agents are the chemical actions promoted in the following cases :—printing a photograph, electroplating a spoon, combustion of coal in a furnace.

4. Stir the parts of a Seidlitz powder together when dry, then throw the mixture into a large beaker half-full of water. What does the result prove?

5. Write your name on a sheet of white paper with a solution of sulphate of iron (copperas), when this is dry dip the paper in solution of ferrocyanide of potash. Repeat the experiment, but use for the writing fluid iodide of potash solution, and for the bath, bichloride of mercury solution. How do you explain the results?

8.—Additional Exercises.

1. Powder some iodide of potash and some bichloride of mercury, then stir the two together.

2. Rub together in a mortar a drop of mercury and a little iodine. If a drop or two of alcohol be added to dissolve the iodine, the combination will be more readily obtained. If the resultant compound is green in colour, add a little more iodine ; if red, add a little mercury.

3. Dissolve a little common salt (sodium chloride), NaCl, and in another test-tube a little silver nitrate, $AgNO_3$; mix the solutions.

4. Heat to redness a piece of bright copper, also a piece of bright iron.

5. Make a mixture of equal parts of powdered nitrate of potash, white sugar and sulphur ; heat a *little* of this on a piece of mica.

6. Heat some nitrate of potash, KNO_3, in a test-tube, until it melts, then drop into it a piece of charcoal about as large as a pea.

7. Repeat experiment 5, sec. 7, but use silver nitrate solution for the writing fluid, then dip the paper into some weak

hydrochloric acid, quickly remove it and expose to bright light for a few minutes. Try the experiment again, and put the paper in a dark drawer after dipping it in the acid. What agent produces the result in this case?

8. Attach a bright piece of iron, three or four inches long, to the terminal wire connected with the zinc of a three or four celled electric battery, and then immerse both the iron and the other terminal wire in a solution of sulphate of copper contained in a glass beaker or clean wooden trough. After a time attach the iron to the other terminal and repeat the experiment.

9. Place on a glass plate a few drops of strong solution of silver nitrate, then place the terminals of the battery in this solution at a distance of about half an inch from each other and hold them still. As the dark solid forms, keep the other terminal moved away from it.

In electrolytic decompositions those substances which are attracted to the positive **electrode** (that is the terminal attached to the copper, carbon or platinum plate), are called **electro-negative**, and those which appear at the negative electrode (the terminal connected with the zinc plate), are **electro-positive**.

CHAPTER III.

1.—Theory of Chemical Action.

From the experiments of the last chapter, it is quite evident that two or more substances may have their parts intimately mixed up with one another, yet each retain its own identity and have all its properties unchanged. In other cases, however, it is quite impossible to observe any trace of either constituent in the resultant substance, and the distinguishing properties of the kinds of matter that were acted on have been altered so that an entirely new material has been formed. It becomes necessary now to give a very brief outline of the theory which offers an explanation of this phenomenon. At the same time, it is well to warn the student that it is only a theory which at present cannot be proved; but it affords a reasonable and consistent explanation of a marvellous number of observed facts, and accounts very generally for the phenomena of chemistry, so that in all probability it is the true theory.

From the observation of both physical and chemical action, it is reasonably certain that all matter, of every state and condition, is made up of separated particles, very minute, indivisible by physical means, yet existing as individual portions. Such particles are called molecules. There are also good reasons for believing that these molecules are in rapid vibration, sometimes moving freely among one another, sometimes so confined that their vibrations may not carry them outside of a limited space. (See High School Physical Science.)

2. In chemistry we have two kinds of matter to deal with—elementary and compound. When the parts that go to make up the molecules are all of one kind, that matter is said to be elementary, because when divided or broken up as much as possible it yields only the one substance. If, however, the individual parts of the molecules are dissimilar, the substance is said to be a compound, because when properly divided up it yields matter of different kinds.

The portions of matter that go to form a molecule are called **atoms.**

Chemical theory further supposes that when combination takes place the atoms of one element join with the atoms of one or more other elements to form groups of atoms all exactly alike in composition ; thus when the magnesium (Chap. I., ex. 1, sec. 2) burned, an atom of the metal united with an atom of oxygen, one of the gases of the atmosphere, to form a group of two atoms, *i.e.,* a molecule, of oxide of magnesium, which is the chemical name of the white ash produced.

Sulphuric acid consists of two atoms of hydrogen, one of sulphur and four of oxygen (these three substances are elements). Now in Chap. I., ex. 3, sec. 3, the chemical action consists in an atom of magnesium crowding out the two atoms of hydrogen that are in every molecule of the acid ; this would manifestly give rise to a molecule different from that of the acid. The hydrogen is a gas, and it was the crowded-out atoms of this element that had congregated into masses, and formed the bubbles of gas that rose to the surface. Had the remaining water been evaporated, a white salt would have been found ; this would have been the matter made up of the new molecules each composed of an atom of magnesium, one of sulphur and three of oxygen.

3. From what has been said, these statements follow :—

> (1) An **atom** is the smallest part of an element that can enter into the composition of a molecule ; hence, that can take part in chemical action.

(2) A **molecule** is the smallest part of a substance, whether elementary or compound, that can have a separate existence.

(3) Molecules are made up of atoms, and, for the same kind of matter, their composition is constant, that is, in all molecules of the same chemical substance there are equal numbers of the same kinds of atoms.

(4) If chemical combination is the union of atoms to form molecules, then decomposition must consist not in the separation of molecules from one another, but in the breaking of them up into atoms or into groups of atoms.

4. **Chemism.**—When masses of the same kind join together to form a single mass it is said that they **cohere**, or that they are held together by **cohesion**. When the substances that join together are of different kinds, they are said to **adhere**. When, however, atoms join together to form molecules, a new force comes into play, which is known as **chemism**, or **chemical affinity**. This differs from both cohesion and adhesion, because it is capable of acting through only infinitesimally short spaces, such as those which separate the molecules of a substance.

We have learnt in the preceding chapter that in very many instances substances will not act chemically among one another, no matter how finely they may be powdered or how intimately mixed, until means are employed to bring the molecules into still closer contact.

Chemical affinity is not equally strong among all substances. Hydrogen and chlorine can scarcely be prevented from combining if mixed, while hydrogen and nitrogen can be made to unite only with the greatest difficulty. Compounds of chlorine and nitrogen, obtained by decomposition of other substances, are held so loosely in union that they are liable to break up with violent explosions, while compounds of chlorine and iron (as well as most other metals), are very stable, that is, are not easily decomposed.

References to chemical affinity may be found: Remsen, 12; Lodge's Modern Views of Electricity, 2nd Ed., 83-4; Muir & Slater, 175: Remsen Theoretical Chem., 14; Tilden, 203; Wurtz, 224, 311.

Atoms and molecules are discussed at length in Ramsay's Chem. Theory for Beginners, p. 61; R. & S., p. 69-80; Wurtz, 33-47, 305-332; Tilden, 3-4, 85; Remsen Th. Chem., 17-18, 36; Muir & Slater, 203-16; Remsen, 68-80.

CHAPTER IV.

1.—Elements.

1. It has been found that by far the greater number of substances with which chemists have to deal are capable of being decomposed into simpler ones. There are, however, about sixty-eight or seventy substances that have never been so divided; these are called elements; and from them, all kinds of matter have been formed, so far as we know at present. It is not likely, though, that these are all the elements, because within late years a number of new ones have been discovered, and it is likely that more will be found out in the future.* On the

---

* Since these lines were written, two English scientists have discovered and isolated a substance that seems to be quite plentiful in the atmosphere, though its presence was not suspected until a few months ago. This substance has been named Argon. As far as investigation has gone at present (Feb'y. 1895) it may be either a new element or a mixture of two or more elements hitherto unknown.

2

other hand, it is quite possible that some of those now treated as elements may be found to be compounds, when methods of research improve and a more exact knowledge of the laws of matter is gained.

2. The following list contains the names, symbols and atomic weights of the sixty-eight elements at present known ; two doubtful ones are omitted :—

NAME OF ELEMENT.	SYMBOL.	ATOMIC WEIGHT.
Aluminium	Al	27·3
Antimony	Sb (Stibium)	122
Arsenic	As	75
Barium	Ba	137
Beryllium	Be	9
Bismuth	Bi	210
Boron	B	11
Bromine	Br	80
Cadmium	Cd	112
Cæsium	Cs	133
Calcium	Ca	40
Carbon	C	12
Cerium	Ce	141
Chlorine	Cl	35·5
Chromium	Cr	52
Cobalt	Co	58·7
Copper	Cu (Cuprum)	63
Didymium	D	147
Erbium	E	166
Fluorine	F	19
Gallium	Ga	70
Germanium	Ge	72·32
Gold	Au (Aurum)	197
Hydrogen	H	1
Indium	In	113·4
Iodine	I	127
Iridium	Ir	193
Iron	Fe (Ferrum)	56
Lanthanum	La	139
Lead	Pb (Plumbum)	207
Lithium	Li	7
Magnesium	Mg	24
Manganese	Mn	55
Mercury	Hg (Hydrargyrum)	200

Name of Element.	Symbol.	Atomic Weight.
Molybdenum	Mo	96
Nickel	Ni	58·7
Niobium	Nb	94
Nitrogen	N	14
Osmium	Os	199
Oxygen	O	16
Palladium	Pd	106·5
Phosphorus	P	31
Platinum	Pt	197·5
Potassium	K (Kalium)	39·1
Rhodium	Ro	104·5
Rubidium	Rb	85·4
Ruthenium	Ru	103·5
Scandium	Sc.	44
Selenium	Se	79·5
Silver	Ag (Argentum)	108
Silicon	Si	28
Sodium	Na (Natrium)	23
Strontium	Sr	87·5
Sulphur	S	32
Tantalum	Ta.	182
Tellurium	Te	128
Thallium	Tl	203·5
Thorium	Th	234
Tin	Sn (Stannum)	118
Titanium	Ti	50
Tungsten	W (Wolfram)	184
Uranium	U	240
Vanadium	V	51
Ytterbium	Yt	173
Yttrium	Y	89·6
Zinc	Zn	65
Zirconium	Zr	89·6

Some of the more important ones are printed in full-faced type.

3. **Metals and Non-Metals.**—These elements are classified into metals and non-metals. The former are characterized by their peculiar appearance (metallic lustre) and by being good conductors of heat and of electricity. It must be remembered, however, that there is no sharp distinction between the two classes. The elements classed as non-metals are hydrogen, bromine,

chlorine, iodine, fluorine, nitrogen, phosphorus, arsenic, boron, carbon, silicon, oxygen, sulphur, selenium, tellurium. Arsenic serves as the connecting link between the metals and non-metals. In appearance, and most of its physical properties, it is metallic, but chemically it is a non-metal because it does not form certain compounds which are characteristic of all true metals.

4. **Symbols.**—In the column headed "Symbols," certain letters are placed opposite the names of the elements. These letters serve as a convenient, short way of indicating the substance; thus, in chemistry, H. stands for hydrogen, Ca. for calcium, Hg. for mercury, and so on through the list. It will be noticed that in most cases the symbols are formed of the first letters of the names of the elements; or, where two or more elements begin with the same letter, the symbol is formed of the initial letter joined with one of the other letters that is prominently sounded in the word; thus, C. stands for carbon, Ca. for calcium, Cd. for cadmium and Cs. for Cæsium. Generally, the names of the elements are formed after the manner of Latin nouns in "um," but in some few cases a popular name has, in ordinary use, supplanted the Latin form; though the symbol is that derived from the Latin word. Iron, copper, silver, mercury, potassium, serve as examples of this.

5. **Atomic Weights.**—By atomic weight of an element is meant the number of times that an atom of the substance is heavier than an atom of hydrogen. Of course it would be absurd to think of weighing out an atom of any substance and comparing its weight with that of an atom of hydrogen. The pupil must understand that these numbers have been derived from the results of a

long series of difficult experiments, which he can not comprehend at the present stage.

Any other element might be adopted as the unit for atomic weight instead of hydrogen ; and if this were done the atomic weights of all the other elements would be relatively changed.

6.—Questions and Exercises.

1. Take a piece of roll sulphur and of iron or copper wire ; hold them, one in each hand, and dip them into a vessel containing boiling water. Note the one along which the heat travels quickest to the hand.

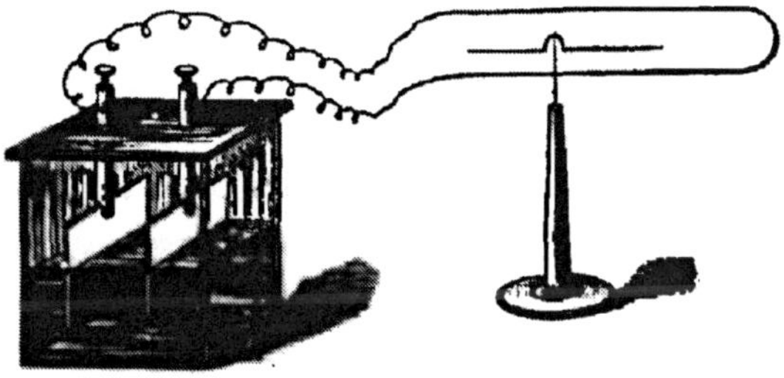

FIG. 4.

2. Insert these same substances, in turn, into the circuit of a galvanic battery. Attach a galvanometer to the circuit, as in Fig. 4, and by its aid note which substance acts as a conductor of electricity. A toy compass will do for the galvanometer.

3. Compare the surface appearance of copper, silver, and other metals with that of sulphur and phosphorus.

4. Connect a galvanometer into a battery circuit, then cut the circuit and dip the cut ends of the wire into a vessel of mercury.

5. What have you noticed which would aid you in classifying mercury as a metal or non-metal ?

For basis of theory of elements, see H. S. Physical Science.

For articles on metals and non-metals, see Muir & Slater's Elementary Chemistry, p. 99 ; Tilden's Chem. Phil., pp. 244-256 ; Roscoe & Schorlemmer, vol. I., pp. 53-4 ; Richter, p. 253 ; Remsen, Inorganic Chem., pp. 452-55 ; D. & W., 12.

CHAPTER V.

1.—To Find out if Water is an Element.

EXPERIMENTS.

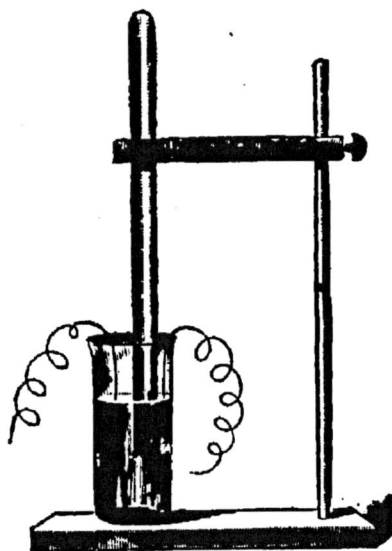

Fig. 5.

1. Take a test-tube about 2 centimetres in diameter, and 10 or 12 centimetres in length. Fill it with acidulated water (1 to 60), and invert it over a beaker containing water. Under the mouth of the test-tube, place the terminal wires of a galvanic battery, as in Fig. 5. The ends of these wires should consist of platinum, and should not touch each other when placed under the mouth of the test-tube.

2. When all the water has been expelled by the accumulated gas in the preceding experiment, raise the tube, keeping it mouth downward, and apply a lighted match to it.

3. Repeat experiment 1, using two test-tubes full of acidulated water, inverted over a soup plate. Place the end of a wire under each tube. Each wire must be insulated where it touches the water, except about 1 centimetre at the end. When gas has filled one of the test-

tubes, stop the current, and examine the gases. Put a glowing splinter of wood into the one with least gas in it, and apply a lighted taper to the full one.

4. Place the battery terminals in acidulated water both in the same vessel. When the gas begins to rise freely, touch the terminals together.

5. Repeat ex. 3, but before applying the splinter and taper turn each tube mouth upwards for a few seconds.

This process of decomposing a compound by making it part of an electric circuit, is called the **Electrolysis** of it, or the *electrolytic decomposition* of it.

2.—Questions and Exercises.

1. Could the gas in the tube in ex. 1, sect. 1, have been produced by decomposition of the battery terminals?

2. Was the gas ordinary air? What reason have you for your answer?

3. How does the mixture of gases differ from each one separately, when tested with a blazing splinter?

CHAPTER VI.

1.—The Preparation and Properties of Hydrogen.

In the preceding chapter it was found that water is a compound made up of at least two substances, which physically resemble each other somewhat, but chemically are quite different. As water is one of the commonest substances known, it has been chosen as a starting point for the study of the chemical properties of matter. Of the two gases of which water is composed, the one that came off in greater quantity, and which burned when brought into the presence of a flame, is known as **hydrogen.** The methods of preparing this gas and the study of its chief properties will occupy the remainder of this chapter.

2.

EXPERIMENTS.

1. Throw a bit of freshly-cut potassium on some water on a plate or in a wide dish. Repeat the experiment, but tinge the water red with litmus solution.

(*a*) Again repeat the experiment in both ways, but use sodium instead of potassium.

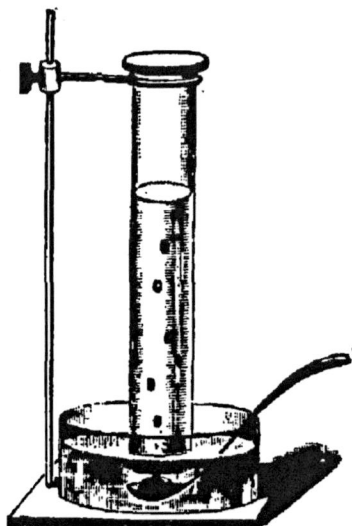

Fig. 6.

2. Confine a bit of sodium or potassium not larger than a pea in a cage of wire gauze, and hold it under a tube that has been inverted full of water over a dish of water, as in Fig. 6. When the sodium has disappeared, another piece may be put in the cage. (If large pieces are used a violent explosion may occur.) When the tube is filled with gas it may be lifted and a lighted taper applied to its mouth.

3. Make a mixture of water and strong sulphuric acid in the proportion of 6 to 1. Fill a test-tube with this mixture, and invert it over a plate containing some of the same mixture. Below the test-tube, which must always be kept with its mouth below the level of the acid and water, place some small pieces of zinc.

3 (a). Vary this experiment by using a piece of magnesium instead of zinc.

Explanation.—Such chemical actions as those between sodium or potassium and water, zinc and sulphuric acid, magnesium and sulphuric acid, come under the class of **substitutions** in which one or more of the atoms of a molecule, generally the hydrogen, are displaced by atoms of other elements.

4. Take a wide-mouthed flask and fit it with a good cork perforated by two glass tubes, one of which passes nearly to the bottom of the bottle, and has on its upper end a funnel-like expansion ; the other tube merely passes through the cork, is bent at right angles, and has a rubber tube attached to it for conveying the gas to a " pneumatic trough," as in Fig. 7. Place some clippings of zinc (or better, some *granulated zinc*, prepared by melting common sheet zinc in an iron ladle, then pouring it from a height of 3 or 4 feet into a pail of cold water), in the bottle, fill it about one-third full of water, and then pour down the funnel

FIG. 7.

tube about one-tenth as much sulphuric acid. The gas begins to form quickly, and is collected in bottles previously filled with water and kept mouth downwards in the water in the pneumatic trough. Collect two or three bottles or large test-tubes full of gas and preserve them for future experiments. Preserve the liquid which remains in the bottle after the gas has ceased to come off. Filter this liquid and either evaporate it over a lamp flame, or allow it to stand in an open vessel for a day or two. Then examine carefully.

5. Keep the mouth of one of the bottles downward, and plunge a lighted taper upward into it. Then withdraw the taper slowly, allowing the burnt end to remain a moment or two at the mouth. Note exactly what phenomena occur (1) just as the taper enters the tube, (2) when the taper is inside the tube, and (3) just as it is withdrawn.

6. Take the second jar, and quickly turn its mouth upwards under the mouth of a similar jar filled with air. Let it remain thus for a few seconds, then apply a burning taper to the mouth of the upper vessel.

7. Pass the gas from the generating apparatus into soap-suds, and set free some bubbles in air.

8. Pass the gas also into a collodion balloon until it is full, then let it free in the air.

Note.—Before collecting this gas, and before bringing a flame near it, be certain that *all air* has been driven out of the generating flask and tubes. To do this allow the gas to escape for a few minutes, then collect a test-tube full over water, as in Fig. 7; bring the test-tube rapidly, mouth downwards, to a lighted lamp. If the gas burns quietly it may be collected, but if there is either a sharp explosion or a whistling sound the air is not all driven out. Neglect of this caution to test the gas in this way will almost certainly lead to violent and very dangerous explosions.

9. Prepare hydrogen gas, using the apparatus Fig. 8 and putting into it granulated zinc and hydrochloric acid. Pass the gas through a tube containing fragments of calcic chloride, for the purpose of drying the gas; and, through the cork which should tightly fit the end of this tube, pass a glass tube drawn to a fine point. After all air has escaped apply a lighted match to the gas-jet.

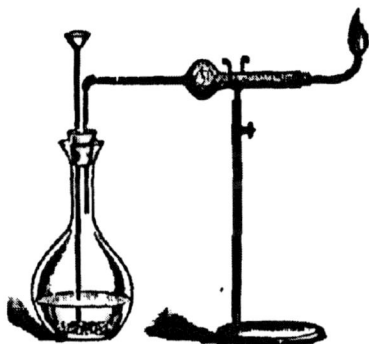

FIG. 8.

10. Introduce a piece of fine iron or steel wire into the flame. Try the effect of the flame on platinum wire and copper wire.

11. *The Chemical Harmonicum.*—Bring down over the jet a tube about 4 centimetres wide and 40 or 50 centimetres long, as in Fig. 9. Use tubes of different diameters and different lengths, and move them slowly up and down.

12. Invert a long, dry, wide-mouthed bottle or bell-jar over the jet.

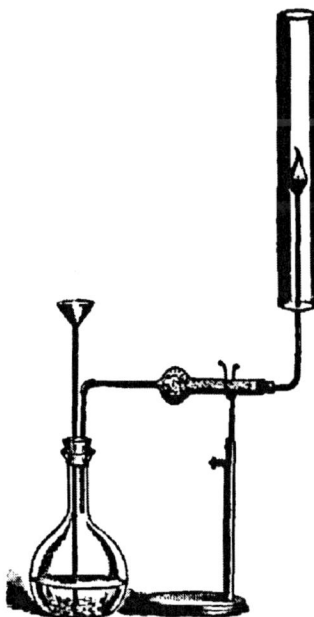

FIG. 9.

13. Have a vessel made out of tin or sheet copper in the form of a double cone, as in Fig. 10. At one end, B, have a neck for a cork, and at the other end, A, a

small opening about one-eighth of an inch in diameter. The vessel should be about five inches long and two and a half inches wide in the middle. Pass a hydrogen delivery tube in through B until the air and hydrogen become well mixed (or fill the vessel with oxygen and hydrogen mixed in a jar), then close B tightly with a cork and hold the end A to a flame. Hold the apparatus so that when the cork blows out no one will be struck.

FIG. 10.

3.—Questions and Exercises.

1. Make a list of the properties of hydrogen which you have observed in the preceding experiments.

2. Compare the phenomena you observed in the cases when sodium and potassium were thrown on water.

3. Float a piece of filtering paper on some water, then drop on this a piece of sodium ; compare the result with that noticed in the first experiment, and also with that of 1 (a) in sec. 2.

4. Heat some water in a metal dish nearly to boiling, then drop into it a little piece of sodium.

Explanation.—Potassium and sodium are two metals that decompose water at ordinary temperatures. Each molecule of water is formed of two atoms of hydrogen and one of oxygen, and one atom of the sodium or of the potassium displaces one of the atoms of the hydrogen, so that instead of the original molecule there is now a new one consisting of one atom of sodium or potassium, one atom of hydrogen and one of oxygen. The displaced atom of hydrogen escapes, and masses of these form the bubbles of gas that rise to the surface when either of these metals is sunk in water. The combustion which goes on in some of the cases when these metals float on the surface of the water, is due to the *hydrogen becoming ignited* on account of the heat generated by the rapidity of the chemical action. The different colours of the flames are owing to small portions of the metals becoming vaporized and burning along with the hydrogen.

5. Try whether the colour of the flame would change if a platinum or copper nozzle were used instead of a glass one, in ex. 9, sec. 2.

6. Is this flame hotter than that of a spirit lamp? Devise some experiment to show that your answer is correct.

7. What phenomena occurred in ex. 11, sec. 2? How was the pitch of the note made to vary? Did the shape of the flame change? How?

8. Where did the moisture on the inside of the bottle, ex. 12 sec. 2, come from? Give a reason for concluding that it could not have come from the generating flask.

9. What became of the zinc in ex. 4, sec. 2? How do you know that the gas was not air?

10. Try if zinc and *strong* sulphuric acid will yield hydrogen. After the gas has ceased to come off, pour the zinc and acid out on a plate, then pick out two or three pieces of the zinc, dry them without rubbing and examine their surfaces; put them in water for a little while, then drop them back into the acid on a part of the plate by themselves. Next try the effect of diluting the acid. Does the hydrogen come from the strong acid or from the water?

11. Point out the resemblances between the gas obtained by the action of zinc and sulphuric acid, sodium and water, and one of those that resulted from the decomposition of water by electricity.

12. If there were two jars, one full of hydrogen and the other full of air, how could you find out which jar contained each gas?

13. What reasons are there for believing that when hydrogen burns, chemical combination is going on?

14. Take two rubber bags, and fill one with hydrogen, the other with oxygen. Subject both bags to an equal amount of pressure between two boards, or otherwise, then connect them with the apparatus known as the oxy-hydrogen blow-pipe, and having turned on the hydrogen, ignite it, then carefully and very gradually turn on oxygen gas from the other bag. A form of blow-pipe apparatus is represented in Fig. 11. Gas holders may be sub-

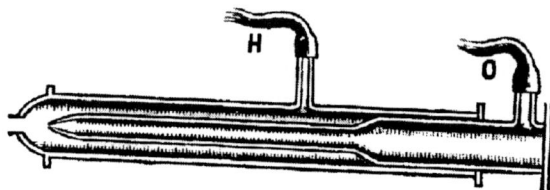

FIG. 11.

stituted for the rubber bags, if more convenient; but the gas should be driven out with considerable force.

15. Introduce into the oxy-hydrogen flame, separately, a piece of platinum wire, of steel, of zinc and of quick-lime.

16. Use an ordinary mouth blow-pipe and connect it with a supply of oxygen by means of a rubber tube; when the gas is escaping under pressure hold the nozzle horizontally in a lamp or gas flame. Try this for heating effect.

17. If sodium forms a compound with water when thrown upon it, where is that compound? Devise an experiment to test the correctness of your answer.

4.—Additional Exercises.

1. To avoid any risk of explosion in the preparation of hydrogen, sodium amalgam may be used instead of sodium. The amalgam is prepared as follows :—Drop into a four or five inch test-tube about a half of a cubic centimetre of mercury, heat this to boiling, then throw into it bits of sodium cut small. Be careful to keep the mouth of the test-tube turned in such a direction that no one will be burned by the hot metal which may spurt out. When sodium, about equal to the mercury in bulk, has been added, pour the liquid quickly out on a cold plate. When cooled there should be a

brittle, silvery white solid,—sodium amalgam. Some of this may be put under the mouth of a test-tube that has been filled with water and inverted as in Fig. 7. Test the gas with a lighted taper, keeping the tube mouth downwards.

2. Try if results similar to those of ex. 1, and 1 (*a*), sec. 2, can be obtained by using ice instead of water.

3. Try if hydrogen is given off in the following cases :—
    (1) Iron is treated with nitric acid.
    (2) Copper is treated with hydrochloric acid.
    (3) Copper   "   " sulphuric "
    (4) Iron   "   "   "   "
    (5) Iron   "   " hydrochloric "
    (6) Zinc   "   " nitric   "

4. A gas jar fitted with a stop-cock is to be pressed mouth downwards into water until about ⅔ of the air is driven out, the stop-cock is then closed and hydrogen equal in volume to about ⅔ of the remaining air pressed into the jar. A delivery tube is then to be fitted to the stop-cock and soap bubbles inflated on a metal dish (an earthenware or glass one will likely be broken) with the mixed gases. By means of a long splinter, ignite the gas in these bubbles. Why should there occur an explosion here, when hydrogen will burn quietly in a jar or at the mouth of a tube ?

5. If some dilute hydrochloric acid be poured on a little carbonate of sodium (washing soda or sal soda) a gas will be generated, is it hydrogen ?

6. Connect a piece of charcoal in a battery circuit in which is also a galvanometer. Compare the conducting power of the charcoal and of a piece of copper wire for electricity, by this means. Compare their conducting powers for heat.

7. Did the gas that arose from the sodium amalgam come from the sodium or the mercury ?

————

5.—Hydrogen and Steam.

As steam is one of the forms into which water may be changed without altering its chemical composition, any result obtained from steam by action between it and another substance is really a result of water acting on that substance.

EXPERIMENTS.

1. Take an iron tube about ¾ of a meter in length and 2 centimeters in diameter (an old gun barrel will do well); fill it nearly full of clean iron filings; fit each end with a tightly-fitting cork and tube, the one leading to a pneumatic trough, the other connected with a flask con-

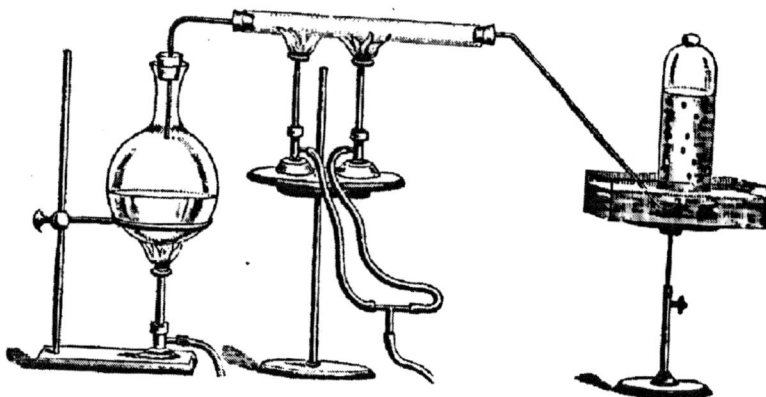

FIG. 12.

taining boiling water, as shewn in Fig. 12. Place the iron tube in a charcoal fire, built upon bricks, or heat it by gas flames. When it is red-hot, boil the water in the flask and force steam through the tube. After the tube has cooled, turn out the iron filings and examine them carefully.

2. Collect a few jars of the gas, prepared in the foregoing manner, and test for hydrogen, as in former experiments.

3. Take a hard glass tube drawn out to a point (such a one as is used for organic analysis with the point

nipped off, is just suitable), and about its middle, place a small quantity of black oxide of copper. Connect it with a tightly-fitting cork and tube to a hydrogen

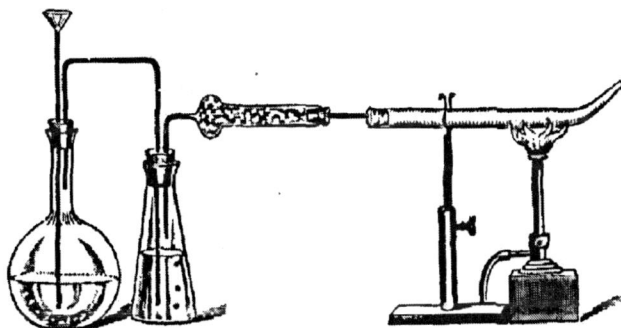

Fig. 13.

generating apparatus. The gas must be dried by passing it through calcic chloride or sulphuric acid, before it reaches the tube with the oxide of copper in it. (See Fig. 13). After allowing the hydrogen to escape for a few minutes, *so as to drive out all the air* from the apparatus, heat the oxide of copper. Condensed vapor of water should pass out of the point of the tube.

What compound is formed in passing steam over red-hot iron in a tube? Compare the action in this case with that of sodium or potassium on water.

Definition.—When the electro-positive element of a compound is freed from some or all of the atoms of the electro-negative element in combination with it, it is said to have been **reduced.**

Note.—The oxide of copper may be introduced at the proper place without smearing the tube by cutting a long narrow strip of paper, folding it up the middle, placing the oxide in the crease thus formed, then gently shoving the paper into the tube and tipping it over so as to spill the powder at the proper place.

3

6—Additional Exercises.

1. Ascertain by experiment whether red-hot copper has the same action on steam that red-hot iron has.

2. Repeat ex. 3, sect. 5, but instead of copper oxide use powdered iron rust, which is an oxide of iron, Fe_2O_3. After the rust has turned black, heat it strongly for some time, then quickly disconnect the combustion tube and spill the black powder in the air. If the experiment is successful the particles should glow brightly as they fall.

3. Try if red oxide of lead can be reduced in the same way that iron oxide is.

4. Compare the phenomena observed when the copper oxide and the iron oxide were heated in the current of hydrogen. How do you account for the change of color in each case?

5. Heat to redness a piece of folded magnesium wire in a current of steam.

6. How do you account for the glowing of the particles of iron when scattered out of the tube after having been reduced? Has the smallness of the particles anything to do with this phenomenon?

7—Classification of Chemical Actions.

For convenience of reference, chemical actions are classified as follows :—

Simple Combination.—When two or more substances unite to form a compound, but without causing the decomposition of any existing compound. Illustrations of this kind of change are found when magnesium burns in air, thus uniting with the oxygen to form magnesic oxide; when oxygen unites with hydrogen to form water, and when sulphur unites with iron to produce sulphide of iron.

Simple Decomposition.—When a compound breaks up into simpler compounds, or into its constituent elements.   Examples of this are seen when mercuric oxide decomposes into mercury and oxygen ; when chlorate of potassium breaks up into oxygen and potassic chloride.

Decomposition by Displacement.—When one or more of the constituents of a compound are displaced by other substances. This occurs when sodium displaces part of the hydrogen of water, and when zinc displaces the hydrogen of sulphuric acid.

Double Displacement.—When two compounds so act on one another that they interchange elements or groups of elements to form two new compounds. This is sometimes known as **metathesis**, and takes place in the case of potassic chloride acting on silver nitrate, $KCl + AgNO_3 = KNO_3 + AgCl$. Sodium carbonate and hydrochloric acid yield sodium chloride and carbonic acid, $Na_2CO_3 + 2HCl = 2NaCl + H_2CO_3$.

Questions and Exercises.

1. Classify the chemical actions of the experiments of sect. 3.

2. Under which class would you place the chemical action when water is decomposed (*a*) by electricity, (*b*) by being passed over red-hot iron; (*c*) by sodium amalgam ?

3. What kind of decomposition goes on when hydrogen is formed from magnesium and dilute sulphuric acid, when hydrogen is formed from iron and hydrochloric acid, when hydrogen is passed over hot iron oxide ?

8.—Notes on Hydrogen.

1. A gram of hydrogen at 760 mm. pressure and 0° C. occupies 11·1636 (11·2 nearly) litres ; hence a litre of hydrogen weighs $\frac{1}{11\cdot1636} = \cdot089578$ (·0896 nearly) grams.

2. The atomic weight of hydrogen is 1, its molecular weight is 2; this means that hydrogen, when freed from combination with other substances, does not continue to exist in the atomic state, but that its atoms unite in groups, and these groups consist each of at least two atoms. Its molecular volume is also 2, which means that each molecule occupies the space of the two atoms of which it is composed, hence there is no condensation in the change into the molecular condition.

3. Hydrogen occurs chiefly in combinations such as water, the acids, the hydrides of many elements, and as a constituent of all organic bodies.

4. Hydrogen when pure is odourless. The disagreeable smell which it has when prepared from zinc is due to impurities of the metal or acid. The chief of these are arsenic, which causes the smell, and lead and carbon which give rise to the black flakes that float on the surface of the acid and water.

5. It has already been shown that potassium and sodium decompose water at ordinary temperatures. The rarer metals barium, strontium and calcium act similarly. Vapour of water led over red-hot iron was decomposed. Zinc, nickel, tin, antimony, lead, bismuth, copper, and some other of the rarer metals will, at a red heat (1000° F.), also decompose steam.

Mercury, silver, gold and platinum do not decompose water at all.

6. Hydrogen is used to aid combustion, for reducing metallic compounds, and for filling balloons. It is one of the mixture of gases which we burn, and which we

call coal gas ; it is freed sparingly when coal is burned in a furnace, and when water is raised to a very high temperature, especially in the presence of red-hot carbon.

CHAPTER VII.

1.—Chemical Notation.

Symbols.—It was stated in a previous chapter, (IV.), that, very generally in chemistry, the symbols of the elements are used instead of the full names. This gives us a kind of chemical shorthand which is brief, expressive, and easily intelligible.

In our present system of chemical notation each symbol stands not only for the name of an element, but also for a definite weight of that element, called its *atomic weight; e.g.*, H always stands for 1 part by weight of hydrogen, and Cl for 35·5 parts by weight of chlorine, hence the symbol of an element stands for three* distinct things :—

   (1) The name of the element ;

   (2) One atom of the element ;

   (3) The atomic weight of the element.

Thus, the symbol O stands for : (1) the name oxygen ; (2) one atom of oxygen ; (3) 16 parts by weight of oxygen.

---

* A symbol stands for these three things taken collectively—not separately. The same emark applies to formulæ.

A small numeral written at the lower right hand corner of a symbol denotes that the atom is doubled, tripled, etc,, *e.g.*, O_2, N_3, P_5.

If we take 1 centigram as our unit of weight, then H signifies 1 centigram of hydrogen, and O, 16 centigrams of oxygen, and so on. O_2 would then represent 32 centigrams of oxygen ; N_3, 42 centigrams of nitrogen : Cl_4, 142 centigrams of chlorine, etc.

Formulæ.—A chemical formula consists of two or more symbols written side by side, and denotes that the elements for which the symbols stand have united to form a chemical compound. The symbol of the most electro-positive constituent of a compound stands first in its formula.

When water was decomposed by electricity, the hydrogen was given off from the electrode that was connected with the *zinc*, or *negative* pole of the battery, and since oppositely electrified bodies attract each other, the hydrogen is said to be more **electro-positive** than the oxygen is.

The formula of a compound substance stands for :

(1) The name of the compound ;
(2) One molecule of the compound ;
(3) The molecular weight of the compound.

The molecular weight of a compound is found by taking the sum of the atomic weights of its constituent elements.

A numeral placed before a formula multiplies every atom and atomic weight in it, as far as the first comma, plus *sign*, or *period*. For example, in $4H_2O$, the 4 multiplies both the atoms and the atomic weights, and means 4 molecules, each consisting of two atoms of hydrogen and one atom of oxygen.

The formula H_2O expresses the following facts :

    (1) That water consists of hydrogen and oxygen ;

    (2) That its molecule consists of 3 atoms : 2 of hydrogen and 1 of oxygen ;

    (3) That its molecular weight is 18.

The formula $C_{12}H_{22}O_{11}$, signifies :

    (1) That cane-sugar consists of carbon, hydrogen, and oxygen ;

    (2) That its molecule consists of 45 atoms : 12 of carbon, 22 of hydrogen, and 11 of oxygen ;

    (3) That its molecular weight is 342.

The molecule, O_2, consists of 2 atoms.

   "   " H_2,   "   "   "

   "   " P_4,   "   4   "

   "   " C_2H_6O, (common alcohol) consists of 9 atoms.

Equations.—A chemical equation consists of signs and formulæ, and expresses the fact that certain substances do, of themselves, or by means of some force applied to them, decompose, and re-arrange their atoms so as to form other substances.

For example the chemical equation—

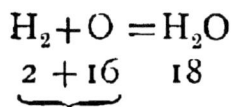

$$H_2 + O = H_2O$$
$$2 + 16 \quad 18$$

expresses the fact that 2 centigrams of hydrogen unite with 16 centigrams of oxygen and form 18 centigrams of water, when a centigram is the unit of weight chosen. The equation is equally true for any other unit of weight, for example, that of one atom of hydrogen.

In the same way, the equation

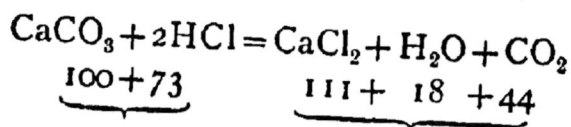

$$CaCO_3 + 2HCl = CaCl_2 + H_2O + CO_2$$
$$\underbrace{100 + 73} \qquad \underbrace{111 + 18 + 44}$$

may be thus translated: mix 100 grams (or ounces) of marble with a solution of 73 grams of hydrochloric acid and they will yield 111 grams of calcic chloride, 18 grams of water, and 44 of carbonic anhydride.

When two symbols or groups of symbols are connected by the sign "+", it means that the substances are mixed, but not in chemical union; when symbols are written side by side without the connecting sign, the meaning is that the substances represented by them are in combination. The sign "=" is not to be understood as used in its algebraic sense of equality; it may be read "gives," or "produces," or "forms." Thus :—

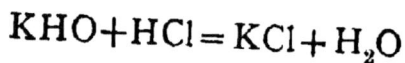

$$KHO + HCl = KCl + H_2O$$

means that the compound consisting of one part of potassium, one part of hydrogen and one part of oxygen when *mixed* with another compound consisting of one part of hydrogen and one of chlorine, may, by proper treatment be made to yield two new compounds which will also be mixed; one of these is made up of one part of potassium and one part of chlorine, the other of two parts of hydrogen and one of oxygen.

The sum of all the atoms of any element on one side of the equation must equal the sum of the atoms of that same element on the other side; hence, the total number of atoms on one side equals the total number on the other, and the sum of the atomic weights on one side is identical with the sum on the other side.

CHAPTER VIII.

1.—Oxygen.

When water was decomposed by electricity two gases were obtained; one of these was oxygen; and this chapter treats of the preparation and the more important properties of this substance.

EXPERIMENTS.

1. Put a couple of grams of chlorate of potash in a test-tube fitted with a cork and delivery tube, as in Fig.

Fig. 14.

14, then heat the tube; when bubbles of gas come off freely, hold a glowing splinter (one that is on fire but not blazing) close to the end of the delivery tube, or better, collect a tube full of the gas, as shown in the figure, and put the splinter in it. When the gas has ceased to come off lift the delivery tube out of the water, then remove the flame from under the tube, and when the latter has cooled, dissolve the white residue; also dissolve a little chlorate of potash separately, test ea' with a drop of silver nitrate solution.

2. Weigh out 1 gram of red oxide of mercury and place in a test-tube fitted with a cork and delivery tube, as in Fig. 14. Heat uniformly at first so as not to break the glass. Oxygen is driven off, and collects in the upright glass vessel standing in the "pneumatic trough." The gas that collects at first should be thrown away. Raise the tube containing the oxygen out of the water and plunge a glowing splinter into it.

Examine with a magnifying glass ϶ grey deposit formed in the test-tube. After gently ᵥ ding out what oxide is still unchanged, strike the mouth of the test-tube sharply on the palm of the hand to drive out some of this grey substance.

3. The best method of preparing oxygen in moderately large quantities in a small laboratory, is the following:—Into a mortar put 10 grams of potassic chlorate and 2½ grams of manganese dioxide. Powder them, and place in a dry Florence flask. Use chemically pure material only, as serious explosions have occurred from

Note.—When a delivery tube from a heated vessel dips under water *never* remove the source of heat until the tube has been lifted out of water, else there will be great danger of the water running into the heated vessel and breaking it if made of glass. Or an explosion might result from the steam suddenly formed if the vessel be made of metal.

organic matter, or carbon being mixed with the manganese dioxide.*

Heat strongly but carefully, and collect four or five small jars of the gas; or better still, collect in a gasholder. Manganese dioxide is mixed with the potassic chlorate to cause the latter to part with its oxygen at a lower temperature than it otherwise would. The manganese dioxide remains unchanged at the end of the experiment.

4. Into a jar of oxygen plunge a piece of glowing charcoal. After combustion has ceased, pour some water into the jar, shake, then test with blue litmus.

5. Put a little sulphur in a deflagrating spoon, ignite, and place in a jar of oxygen. Pour some water into the jar after the combustion has ceased. Test with blue litmus paper; also taste the solution.

6. Draw the temper from a piece of fine watch spring by passing it slowly through a lamp flame; file the end of the spring very thin, then tip with sulphur, or better, wrap the thin end of the spring tightly round a piece of charcoal, and ignite. Place in a jar of oxygen, and it will burn with beautiful scintillations. Add water to the solid that forms, then taste and test, first with

---

*To test the manganese dioxide heat a little of it on a deflagrating spoon; if any glowing or combustion is observed there are dangerous impurities in it.

Note.—To make red and blue solutions, "steep some solid litmus in water or weak alcohol. Divide the liquid which you pour off from the sediment, into two parts; to one add a few drops of weak sulphuric acid; to the other add a little solution of caustic soda. You will then have red and blue litmus solutions, and if you add them to the products of your experiments with oxygen, you will be able to test whether a new compound has been formed in case other evidence of a chemical change is wanting."

Litmus paper is prepared by dipping strips of white filtering paper in these solutions, and allowing them to dry.

blue litmus, then with red litmus, being careful to see that the results are not masked by the combustion products of the carbon or sulphur. Observe closely the deposit on the sides of the jar, and examine the pellets that fell to the bottom.

7. Clean the spoon used in the last experiment, and place a piece of phosphorus on it about the size of a pea. Ignite, and place in a jar of oxygen. After combustion has ceased, remove the spoon, and pour some water into the jar. Shake up the water with the product of the combustion, taste, and then add some blue litmus solution.

8. Place a small piece of sodium in a deflagrating spoon, hold it in a lamp flame until it begins to burn, and then plunge into a jar of oxygen. Add water, taste, and test with reddened litmus.

9. Pour a little potassium hydroxide into a jar of oxygen. Shake, and if no change in volume takes place, add a small quantity of pyrogallic acid. Shake again, and note any change. Modify this experiment by selecting two test-tubes such that one will just pass mouth first into the other, fill the smaller one with oxygen gas and half fill the larger with solution of caustic potash ; drop into this as much pyrogallic acid as will rest on a 10 cent piece, and quickly pass the other tube mouth first into it ; let the whole stand for some hours.

10. Make a large bubble on a plate with oxygen gas, then hold a magnet near it. Does the magnet attract the bubble film, or the oxygen in the bubble? Devise an experiment to determine this point.

2.—Tests.

1. If free oxygen be present to any considerable extent a glowing splinter will rekindle when put into the gas.

2. If copper clippings be heated with weak nitric acid and the resultant gas allowed to stand over water it will become colourless. Oxygen passed into this gas causes it to turn brown and be dissolved in water.

3. A mixture of pyrogallic acid and caustic potash solutions (pyrogallate of potash) will turn dark brown in presence of oxygen.

3.—Questions and Experiments.

1. How would you separate manganese dioxide from the other ingredients as it occurs in the residue from the preparation of oxygen? How would you show that there is a substance in this residue different from either of those taken at first?

2. Point out the resemblances and differences you have observed between oxygen and hydrogen.

3. Oxygen is said to support combustion much more energetically than air does. What reasons are there for such a statement as this?

4. When charcoal or sulphur is burned in oxygen, the gases produced differ from air. How may this difference be shown?

4.—Notes.

Oxygen: atomic weight, 16; mol. weight, 32; mol. vol. 2; specific weight (air=1) 1·10563.

Oxygen occurs free in the atmosphere, of which it forms about 21% by volume; it also exists largely in combination, as in water, in many minerals, and in all organic bodies.

Oxygen is one of the substances entering into most chemical actions that are known as combustion, and is the gas necessary for the support of life.

It is possible that in the preparation of oxygen from chlorate of potash and manganese dioxide the latter substance may act by absorbing oxygen from the chlorate to form a higher oxide, Mn_2O_7, which on account of its instability is immediately decomposed. There are other substances which may be substituted for the MnO_2 in this operation, viz.:—CuO, Fe_2O_3 and PbO. Some of these, at least, are capable of being further oxidized to CuO_2, PbO_2; (R. & S. I., 174). The object of using the MnO_2 is to cause the oxygen to be given off at a temperature much lower than if the chlorate were heated alone, hence it exerts some effect which causes the molecules of the chlorate to be decomposed more readily.

When iron is burned in oxygen the black brittle globules that fall to the bottom are magnetic oxide of iron; they have the composition Fe_3O_4 and are generally considered to be a union of FeO_2 and Fe_2O_3, ferrous and ferric oxides respectively, hence sometimes called ferro-ferric oxide. The red powder which settles on the side of the jar is ferric oxide, Fe_2O_3. Oxygen may be separated from other gases with which it is mixed by using pyrogallate of potash.

5.—Additional Exercises.

1. Heat some red oxide of lead in the same manner as in experiment 2, sec. 1. Test as before.

2. Cut zinc foil into fine strips, tip them with sulphur, place on a small piece of sheet zinc on a cork; ignite and place in a jar of oxygen. After combustion has ceased, add water to the compound formed, then taste and test with litmus paper.

3. Repeat experiment 8, sec. 1, using, first, potassium, and then magnesium.

4. Burn a piece of charcoal in a jar of oxygen, then shake some lime water up with the gas that is in the jar. Shake some lime water up with oxygen. What does this demonstrate? Does a similar result follow from the burning of sulphur in oxygen?

5. Stir some red lead with dilute nitric acid, after a brown powder, PbO_2, peroxide of lead, has formed, filter, dry the powder, and try if, when heated, it will yield oxygen.

Fig. 15.

6. Bend a piece of wire into the form shown in Fig. 15, place a piece of phosphorus about as big as a pea on top of it, then set it on a plate of water and place a bell jar filled with oxygen over it. Let it stand for two or three days, being careful that there is plenty of water on the plate. Then test the water with litmus paper.

7. Try if nitrate of potash (saltpetre) when heated gives off oxygen. When the nitrate begins to boil, drop into it a bit of charcoal or the end of a match.

8. Mix some manganese dioxide with sulphuric acid and heat gently in a test-tube. Determine if oxygen is given off. Pass the gas that comes off through cold water, and test again for oxygen.

9. When copper oxide was heated in a current of hydrogen what happened? Try if the operation can be reversed by heating some fine copper filings in a current of oxygen.

10. Place some zinc filings in a hard glass tube, heat this while a current of oxygen is passing through it. Repeat the experiment, using lead filings.

Note.—A bell jar full of gas may easily be transferred from one place to another by covering the mouth with a piece of ground glass.

6.—Ozone.

EXPERIMENTS.

1. Suspend a stick of clean phosphorus in a closed bottle that has a little water in the bottom of it ; let the phosphorus remain for a couple of days, then remove the stopper and smell the gas in the bottle. (If the phosphorus is covered with a brown coating scrape this off under water.)

2. Repeat the experiment and test the gas formed in the bottle, with starch paper, prepared as follows :—

Boil some starch to a paste, drop into it some potassic iodide, dip in this strips of white unsized paper (strips from a leaf of a scribbler will answer). Hold one of these test papers in ozone.

3. In a wide-mouthed bottle or beaker put two grams of crystals of permanganate of potash, $KMnO_4$, and on these pour some sulphuric acid, but do *not warm* the mixture. Test the gas with the starch paper. Smell the gas.

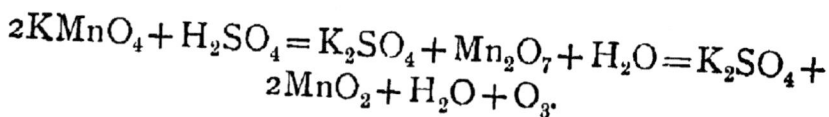

$$2KMnO_4 + H_2SO_4 = K_2SO_4 + Mn_2O_7 + H_2O = K_2SO_4 + 2MnO_2 + H_2O + O_3.$$

4. When the gas is coming off freely from the mixture of permanganate and sulphuric acid, hang in it, but so as not to touch the liquid, a piece of paper saturated with turpentine. This should burst into flame after a short time.

Note.—Care must be taken to keep this mixture well cooled as Mn_2O_7, manganese heptoxide, explodes violently when heated. The beaker containing the mixture should be set in a larger vessel of water.

5. Fit up a bottle and three test-tubes, as shown in Fig. 16; into the bottle put a mixture of permanganate of potash and sulphuric acid, and into one test-tube a faintly blue solution of indigo, into a second a weak solution of logwood, and into the third a slightly purple solution of permanganate of potash; allow the gas that comes off to bubble through the three solutions for a few hours.

FIG. 16.

6. Pass some of the gas prepared, as in the last experiment, through a solution of iodide of potassium, KI.

Explanation. — The gas formed in these experiments is **ozone**. The symbol for it is usually written O_3, but better OO_2. Chemically it is oxygen, but it has properties which ordinary oxygen has not. This may be demonstrated by using oxygen instead of ozone in Ex. 4, 5 and 6. The theory is, that ozone exists in a molecular state different from that of oxygen; for theoretically, while the molecule of oxygen consists of two atoms, that of ozone consists of three. This three-atom molecule is very unstable, so is easily decomposed into ordinary oxygen. Thus, $2O_3 = 3O_2$; but as each molecule of O_3 breaks up, one atom is set free as an atom, not as a molecule. The subsequent union of two of these free atoms forms the third molecule.

An **Oxide** is a compound formed by the union of oxygen with some other element.

4

7.—Additional Exercises.

1. Pass the gas prepared, as described in Fig. 16, into some sulphuric ether, after a time pour a little of this ether into weak solutions of indigo, logwood and litmus. Try if the ether before its treatment with the gas will produce the same effect on these substances.

2. Pass sparks between the terminals of an electric machine in dry air, after a little while the odour of ozone should be detected.

3. Try if ozone will support combustion as oxygen does by causing a glowing splinter to burst into flame.

References for ozone, R. & S., vol. I., 194-201 ; Muir & Slater, 224 ; R., 85-90.

CHAPTER IX.

Hydrogen Dioxide.

Hydrogen and oxygen form two compounds ; one of these has already been considered in Chapter v., the other is hydrogen dioxide, or hydrogen peroxide, and it is intended to discuss this substance in the present chapter. Its formula is H_2O_2.

1.—Hydrogen Peroxide.

Barium oxide, BaO, when heated to dull redness in a current of oxygen, or in a free supply of air, changes into barium dioxide, BaO_2.

EXPERIMENTS.

1. Treat some barium peroxide, BaO_2, with hydrochloric acid diluted with two or three times its own bulk

of water ; after the white oxide has all dissolved, drop in some sulphuric acid, and when the precipitate ceases to form, filter. The filtrate is a solution of hydrogen dioxide. As this is a very unstable compound it cannot be evaporated in the ordinary way by heating, because it then decomposes into water and oxygen.

$$BaO_2 + 2HCl = BaCl_2 + H_2O_2.$$

The sulphuric acid was added to form an insoluble compound with the barium chloride, $BaCl_2$, which then separated from the liquid as a precipitate.

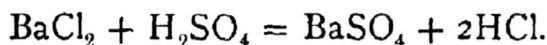

$$BaCl_2 + H_2SO_4 = BaSO_4 + 2HCl.$$

The solution of hydrogen dioxide may be evaporated under an air pump, if required.

2. Divide the solution of hydrogen dioxide into a number of parts, into one drop some logwood solution, into another some indigo, into a third some litmus.

3. Prepare some test papers as directed for ozone, and dip one of them into hydrogen dioxide solution. If it does not turn blue at once add a few drops of clear ferrous sulphate (copperas), $FeSO_4$, solution. Dip another piece of the paper into another part of the hydrogen dioxide solution, and let it stand for several hours.

4. Make an acid solution of potassium permanganate, $KMnO_4$, but only slightly purple in colour, add hydrogen dioxide solution and shake the two together, then let the mixture stand for some time. Try if the permanganate solution loses colour when no hydrogen dioxide is added to it.

5. Heat a portion of this hydrogen dioxide solution in a corked test-tube; place a strip of the test paper above the solution to find if this compound comes off as gas. After heating, test the liquid with the test paper and ferrous sulphate solution.

Explanation.—The chemical action of hydrogen peroxide is due to the same cause as that of ozone, viz.: the weak chemical attraction existing between one of the oxygen atoms and the other parts of the molecule, that is, H_2O. Whatever may be the molecular structure of the group of atoms, it is clear from the result of its decomposition that one atom of oxygen is held very loosely, hence easily breaks away from the others as an atom. These loose atoms join in pairs to form oxygen molecules, thus :—$H_2O_2 = H_2O + O$ or better, $2H_2O_2 = 2H_2O + O_2$.

3.—Additional Experiments.

1. Will barium dioxide, when treated with dilute sulphuric acid, yield hydrogen dioxide?

2. Try if barium dioxide, when treated with dilute nitric acid, and the result precipitated with a few drops of sulphuric acid, will give a solution of hydrogen dioxide?

3. Does the manner of the decomposition of the hydrogen dioxide molecule indicate in any way that the formula should be written H_2O_2, rather than as two hydroxyl molecules, $2HO$?

CHAPTER X.

Nascent State.

Many substances, particularly elements, at the instant at which they are freed from combination, possess a chemical activity in the way of forming molecules which requires a special explanation. This will be briefly given in the present chapter.

Ordinary oxygen does not bleach indigo, logwood, litmus or permanganate of potash solutions, yet ozone, which is only oxygen in a somewhat altered molecular combination, does destroy the colours of these substances.

Hydrogen gas may be led for days, through silver chloride held in suspension in water, yet the chloride will not be decomposed. If, however, some silver chloride (prepared by dropping hydrochloric acid, or a solution of a chloride, into a solution of silver nitrate) be spread on a piece of zinc and the whole immersed in dilute sulphuric acid, the silver chloride will, in a few hours, be reduced to metallic silver, (1). $Zn + H_2SO_4 = ZnSO_4 + 2H$. (2). $H + AgCl = HCl + Ag$. Similarly, a current of hydrogen passed through potassic chlorate solution has no effect on it, but hydrogen generated in the solution from some pieces of zinc and dilute sulphuric acid will reduce the chlorate to the chloride of potassium, $Zn + H_2SO_4 = ZnSO_4 + 2H$, and $6H + KClO_3 = KCl + 3H_2O$ Free hydrogen has no effect on nitric acid, but hydrogen freed in presence of the acid from a compound, at once reduces the acid, (1). $Zn + 2HNO_3 = Zn (NO_3)_2 + 2H$. (2). $2H + 2HNO_3 = 2H_2O + 2NO_2$. This is the reason that zinc and nitric acid do not yield free hydrogen but an oxide of nitrogen generally. Many substances in solution are oxidized by passing chlorine gas through the liquid. Now chlorine contains no oxygen, so we are obliged to look elsewhere for a reason for this change. It is well known that chlorine has a great affinity for hydrogen; so strong indeed is this attraction, that it breaks up the water molecules, appropriates the hydrogen for the formation of hydrochloric acid, and sets the oxygen free, and it is this latter which oxidizes the substances, $2Cl + H_2O = 2HCl + O$, though a stream of oxygen gas produces no such effect. Numerous instances might be given of similar chemical action brought about by elements at the instant at which they are freed from combination, though they do not retain the power for any appreciable length of time. When the molecule of a compound is decomposed, the constituents pass off as atoms, and these may either unite with other elements to form new combinations, or may remain uncombined with any other substance; but in the latter case they combine with each other, and, since the combining powers of atoms are limited in amount, though for different elements these amounts are different, it follows that if two atoms of the same kind combine with each other their affinity for other atoms is lessened by the amount of attraction by which they are held together. Their chemical activity in the way of forming new combinations will therefore be reduced; hence, at the instant at which atoms are freed from molecules and exist as individual atoms, their chemical attraction for other atoms is stronger than it is after they have joined in groups. At the time at which a portion of an element exists as atoms, and before these have combined to form molecules, it is said to be in the **nascent state.** When the molecule of ozone breaks up into a molecule of oxygen and an atom of oxygen, the latter is in the nascent condition, that is, uncombined with any other atom, so that its powers of combination are not impaired in any way. On this account it oxidizes, and thus destroys the colouring matters spoken of; unites so vigorously with turpentine that combustion is set up, $C_{10}H_{16}+28O_3 = 10CO_2+8H_2O+28O_2$; and decomposes potassic iodide by oxidizing the potassium, $O_3+2KI = O_2+K_2O+I_2$. Similarly the hydrogen atoms when first liberated decompose silver chloride, reduce nitric acid, reduce potassic chlorate and decompose sulphuric acid under proper conditions. The *nascent* oxygen resulting from the spontaneous decomposition of the hydrogen peroxide molecule, or from the action of chlorine on the water molecule, acts in a way precisely similar to that in which the oxygen did, when the ozone molecule was broken up.

For more detailed treatment, see Tilden, p. 125-6; Wurtz, p. 207-8; Muir and Slater, p. 233; Remsen, Th. Ch. 50; R., 90; D. and W., 69.

CHAPTER XI.

ACIDS, BASES AND SALTS.

It has been necessary several times to mention substances which have been called **acids.** These form one of three classes that include a great many chemical compounds. The other two classes are **bases** and **salts.**

Salts and acids are always compounds; bases also are compounds, and are either oxides or hydroxides of metals. Oxides of the non-metals are generally acid-forming substances,—never bases; and the hydroxides of the non-metals are acids.

Hydroxides or **hydrates** are compounds formed by the union of an oxide with water.

1.—Acids.

In order to learn some of the general properties of acids, perform the following experiments, using any three or four substances labelled acids, which you can find upon your working table :—

1. Pour some of the acid, or drop a crystal about as big as a pea if the acid is a solid, into twenty or thirty times its own volume of water in a test-tube. Taste the solution.

2. Half-fill a small test-tube with blue litmus solution and add to it some of the diluted acid. Add some of the acid to some red litmus solution also.

3. Place some "bread soda," bicarbonate of sodium, $NaHCO_3$, in a test-tube and pour some of the dilute acid upon it.

Tabulate your results as follows :—

Name of Acid.	Taste.	Action on Red Litmus.	Action on Blue	So	REMARKS.

All acids contain replaceable hydrogen; that is, hydrogen which may be driven out of the molecule by one or more atoms of some other substance. A familiar example is in the preparation of hydrogen gas from sulphuric acid, in which two hydrogen atoms are replaced by one of zinc.

2.—Bases.

Any metallic oxide or hydroxide, the metal of which is capable of replacing the hydrogen of an acid is a base. The hydrogen of acids may also be replaced by metals, the term base, however, is usually applied only to the oxides and hydrates. The latter require a little attention. A molecule of an hydroxide is formed by the union of a metallic atom with one or more hydroxyl groups (HO). Examples of these have already been met with when potassium and sodium were thrown on water. These hydrates are formed either by direct action of the metal on water (this occurs only with some of the alkalies) or by dissolving the oxide in water. (There is a third method which need not be discussed here, as it belongs essentially to the chemistry of the metals).

EXPERIMENTS.

1. Take a piece of the metal potassium, about the size of a pea, place it in an iron spoon, and heat it over a spirit lamp until it has ceased to burn. Then add a little water, and test the solution with red, and with blue litmus, as before. Taste the solution.

2. Repeat this experiment, using the metals, magnesium and sodium.

3. Obtain a piece of quick lime, place a bit of it on a piece of dry litmus paper; then put a piece of the lime as big as a bean in a large test-tube full of water, shake it up, and let the whole stand until the water becomes clear. Taste it, and test with litmus and with turmeric paper.

4. Repeat, using barium oxide.

Tabulate results as in the case of the acids.

3.—Salts.

When the hydrogen of an acid is replaced by a metal, or the metal of a base, the resulting compound is a salt.

EXPERIMENTS.

1. Take a piece of "caustic soda" (sodic hydrate) NaHO, about the size of a pea, and dissolve it completely in a test-tube of water, then add to it hydrochloric acid, drop by drop, until a piece of blue litmus paper placed in the solution slowly begins to turn red, pour half of this solution into an evaporating dish, place on a sand bath and heat until all the water is driven off. Carefully examine the residue. Taste it.

Pour the rest of the solution into a flat dish of any kind, and allow it to remain for a day or two in a warm room.

2. Perform similar experiments using potassium hydroxide, KHO (caustic potash), and nitric acid; also sodium hydroxide and sulphuric acid.

3. Use the acids as in the last experiment, but instead of the base take copper or zinc.

Tabulate your results, especially with regard to their effect on litmus.

Acids in which there is one replaceable hydrogen atom are **monobasic**. Nitric, hydrochloric and acetic acids are examples. These have the formulæ HNO_3, HCl, $HC_2H_3O_2$ respectively. Those acids in which there are two atoms of replaceable hydrogen are **dibasic**. Sulphuric, H_2SO_4, and carbonic, H_2CO_3, acids are examples. Either one or both atoms of the hydrogen may be replaced, thus forming either **acid** or **neutral** salts; thus

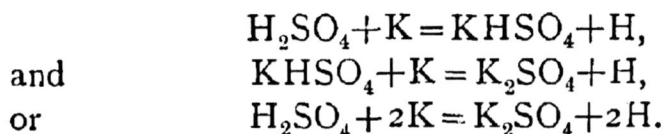

$$H_2SO_4 + K = KHSO_4 + H,$$
and
$$KHSO_4 + K = K_2SO_4 + H,$$
or
$$H_2SO_4 + 2K = K_2SO_4 + 2H.$$

Of course such salts are possible only when the valency of the base is less than the **basicity** of the acid ;—the basicity being determined by the number of atoms of replaceable hydrogen in the molecule.

Acids with three atoms of replaceable hydrogen are **tribasic**. Phosphoric acid H_3PO_4, is a good example of this class. Either one, two or three of its hydrogen atoms may be displaced, and these not necessarily by the same base, thus :—

NaH_2PO_4, Na_2HPO_4, Na_3PO_4, $Ca(H_2PO_4)_2$, $NaNH_4HPO_4$

are some of the salts formed from it.

EXPERIMENTS.

1. When nitric acid is prepared, a difficultly soluble, white solid was left in the retort; procure a lump of this, wash it for a minute or two in a stream of water to free it from any sulphuric acid that might be adhering to it,

then dissolve it. Test a part of the solution (1) with litmus, (2) with a solution of barium nitrate,—the former shows the acid nature of the solution, the latter that it is a sulphate. To the part of the solution left add, cautiously, caustic potash until it is neutralized, then evaporate to dryness. A white salt should be obtained which answers to the test for a sulphate but is neutral to litmus.

2. Weigh out three and a half grams of strong sulphuric acid, and separately 2 grams of solid potassic hydrate, dissolve the latter in a measuring glass. Add half the potash solution to the whole of the acid, evaporate to dryness, dissolve the salt and test a drop of the solution with litmus and with barium chloride. Add the rest of the potash solution, again evaporate to dryness and test as before. This time the salt should be neutral to litmus.

In naming them, acid salts are frequently distinguished from neutral ones by the prefix bi-, thus, $NaHSO_4$ and $NaHCO_3$ are known as acid sulphate and acid carbonate of sodium, bisulphate and bicarbonate of sodium, or sodium hydrogen sulphate and sodium hydrogen carbonate.

These experiments show that it is possible to replace the hydrogen of sulphuric acid in two separate stages, and that two distinct substances are obtained as a result of these displacements. These illustrate the double basicity of the acid. A similar attempt with potassic hydrate and nitric acid will result in only one salt being formed, hence nitric acid is monobasic.

There is still another class of salts known as **basic**, but, as there will be no occasion to refer to them in this book, all discussion of them will be omitted.

4.—Questions and Exercises.

1. Given the acids HNO_3, H_2CO_3, and copper, potassium, sodium hydrate and silver, write the formulæ for all the salts that theoretically could be formed. Write the names of these salts.

2. Which one out of each of the following pairs is correct and why? (1) $PbNO_3$ or $Pb(NO_3)_2$; (2) $ZnHSO_4$ or $ZnSO_4$; (3) $NaSO_4$ or $NaHSO_4$; (4) $AgSO_4$ or Ag_2SO_4.

3. From what acid is each of the following prepared, and what is its basicity, as shown by the salt? KNO_2, $Pb(NO_2)_2$, Na_2SO_3, $CaSO_4$, $Ba(NO_3)_2$.

CHAPTER XII.

Chemical Nomenclature.

The object of this chapter is to explain the principles upon which the names of the compounds in inorganic chemistry are based. To the beginner these names doubtless appear bewildering in their variety, but a single lesson, or at most two lessons, should put him in a position to readily name the inorganic compounds, once he knows a few formulæ, (chiefly of acids), and the valency of the elements and radicals.

1.

Binary compounds, that is, those of two elements, have names that end in -ide. The most electro-positive element stands first (which one this is, will be learned by practice), and its name may be in either the noun or adjectival form in the complete designation. Thus KCl is potassic chloride, potassium chloride or chloride of potassium; H_2S is hydric sulphide, hydrogen sulphide or sulphide of hydrogen.

When the electro-negative element unites in more than one proportion with the other, the number of parts of it in any particular combination are indicated by the prefixes **mono** or **mon-**, **di-**, **tri-**, **tetr-**, or **tetra-**, and **pent-**. Thus H_2O (water) is chemically hydric monoxide; H_2O_2 is hydrogen dioxide; CO is monoxide of carbon; CO_2 is carbon dioxide; PCl_3 is phosphorus trichloride; CCl_4 is carbon tetrachloride; P_2O_5 is phosphorus pentoxide. An old ending, **-uret**, is sometimes used instead of **-ide**; and **prot-** is an old prefix used instead of **mono-**.

In the names of acids the endings **-ous** and **-ic** very generally occur, and they indicate that the acid whose name ends in **-ic** has in its composition a greater quantity of oxygen than the one whose name ends in **-ous**. This does not mean that either of these endings points to a fixed quantity of oxygen, but that relatively the -ous acid always has in it less oxygen than the -ic acid. Thus HNO_3 is nitric acid, and HNO_2 nitrous acid; $HClO_2$ chlorous acid, $HClO_3$ chloric acid; H_2SO_3 sulphurous acid, and H_2SO_4 sulphuric acid. The prefixes **hypo** (beneath) and **per** (above) are used also with regard to the quantity of oxygen in the molecule of the acid. Thus HClO is hypochlorous acid; $HClO_2$ chlorous acid; $HClO_3$ chloric acid, and $HClO_4$ perchloric acid.

In naming salts the prefixes belonging to the names of the acids are preserved, but in the salt the ending -ous of the acid is changed into -ite, and the ending ic- of the acid into -ate. Thus $KClO$ is hypochlorite of potassium; $NaClO_2$ chlorite of sodium; $AgClO_3$ chlorate of silver, and $KClO_4$ perchlorate of potassium; $CaSO_4$ is sulphate of calcium, and $Cu(NO_2)_2$ is nitrite of copper. In salts the adjectival form of the name of the base may be used. Thus $AgSO_3$ is argentic sulphite, or silver sulphite, or sulphite of silver; KNO_3 is potassic nitrate, potassium nitrate or nitrate of potassium.

CHAPTER XIII.

1.—Valency or Atomicity.

The student who has followed this book thus far will probably have had some difficulty in deciding in what proportions elements unite with one another. The object of this chapter is to explain this difficulty, as far as can be done at this elementary stage.

The following are the formulae of some well known compounds:—

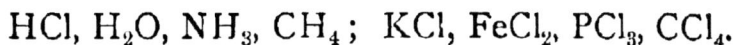

HCl, H_2O, NH_3, CH_4; KCl, $FeCl_2$, PCl_3, CCl_4.

In the first four, hydrogen unites in proportions of one, two, three and four atoms with one atom respectively of chlorine, oxygen, nitrogen and carbon. The second group shows similar compounds of chlorine. It seems, therefore, that one atom of hydrogen unites with one atom of chlorine to form a definite stable compound, while it takes two atoms of hydrogen to form such a compound with one of oxygen, three atoms of hydrogen with one of nitrogen, and four of hydrogen with one of carbon. Just as hydrogen is taken as the unit of atomic weight, so it is taken here as the unit of combining power, and the other elements are *valued* with reference to this one. Thus an element, one atom of which unites with one atom of hydrogen, or replaces an atom of hydrogen in combination is said to be a **univalent** or a **monad** element, that is, it is worth one. Similarly an element, one of whose atoms is capable of uniting with two atoms of hydrogen, or of replacing two atoms of hydrogen in a compound, is called a **bivalent** or **diad** element,—worth two. According to this classification elements are divided into **monad** or **univalent**, **diad** or **bivalent**, **triad** or **trivalent**, **tetrad** or **tetravalent**, **pentad** or **quinquivalent**, and **hexad** or **hexevalent** elements. The combining forces of an atom of an element, or its replacing power, in terms of the number of atoms of hydrogen with which it unites or which it displaces, is known as its **valency** or **atomicity**. Even for the same element this valency is frequently a variable quantity. The reasons for this cannot be considered until a later stage, but a few examples will make clear its importance. H_2O and H_2O_2 are both compounds of hydrogen and oxygen ; sulphur and oxygen form SO_2 and SO_3 ; carbon and oxygen unite to produce the oxides CO and CO_2 ; FeO, Fe_2O_3

and Fe_3O_4 are three oxides of iron; and of lead and oxygen we have the compounds PbO, Pb_2O_3, Pb_3O_4 and PbO_2.

Monads unite with one another in the proportion of one to one; diad elements also unite with one another in the proportion of one to one, but with monads in the proportion of one to two.

If there are six elements whose valencies are indicated by the Roman numerals, (the common way of marking it), and whose names are represented by letters, thus, A^i, B^{ii}, C^{iii}, D^{iv}, E^v, F^{vi}, they may form combinations as follows: A_2B, A_3C, A_4D; C_2B_3, B_2D, E_2B_5, B_3F, D_3C_4, etc.

It must not be inferred from what is said above that every element is capable of uniting with every other one. There are many cases in which two elements have never been known to unite directly with each other, or to form a group from the breaking down of higher compounds; examples are, oxygen and fluorine, potassium and sodium, hydrogen and bismuth.

Artiads.—Atoms of elements of even atomicity are termed artiads.

Perissads.—Atoms of elements of uneven or odd atomicity are called perissads.

The sum of the atomicities of the elements in a compound is always an even number; and when an element has more than one valency it changes two degrees at a time, so that an element can never be both an artiad and perissad.

5

2.

The following table gives the valency of the principal elements. It will be found useful to commit it to memory :—

	MONADS.	DYADS.	TRIADS.	TETRADS.	PENTADS.	HEXADS.
NON-METALS.	Bromine. Chlorine. Fluorine. Hydrogen. Iodine.	Oxygen. Sulphur.	Boron. Nitrogen. Phosphorus. Arsenic.	Carbon. Silicon. Sulphur.	Nitrogen. Phosphorus. Arsenic.	Sulphur.
METALS.	Potassium. Sodium. Silver.	Calcium. Copper. Magnesium Mercury. Manganese. Strontium. Zinc. Iron. Barium. Lead.	Antimony. Bismuth. Gold. Aluminium.	Aluminium Cobalt. Iron. Lead. Manganese. Nickel. Platinum. Tin.	Antimony. Bismuth.	Chromium. Manganese. Iron.

Many of the elements do not unite directly with hydrogen ; when this is the case their atomicities are calculated from their union with other elements whose combinations with hydrogen are known.

3.—Radicals.

In many cases a group of atoms acts in combination and replacement in the same way that single atoms do.

An example of this we have already met in the hydroxyl group HO, which unites with potassium and sodium to form the hydrates of these metals.

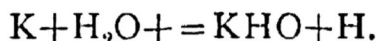

$$K+H_2O+ = KHO+H.$$

These *compound radicals*, as they are called, do not exist in the free state, but when separated in the decomposition of compounds, they unite either with each other or with some other substance present.

4.—Equivalent.

Chemical equivalent is a term used to express the proportions, by weight, in which elements combine with one another, or displace one another in a compound, one part, by weight, of hydrogen being taken as the unit. Thus, the chemical equivalents of oxygen, sulphur, chlorine and nitrogen are respectively 8, 16, 35·5, 4·66.

Chemical equivalents must not be confounded with combining proportions. The former is taken with reference to hydrogen only; the latter may be taken with reference to any other element. Thus from CH_4 we get the equivalent of carbon, but from CO, and CO_2, are obtained the two proportions in which carbon and oxygen combine.

References for this chapter.—D. & W., 192; Tilden, 139; Richter, 169; R., 81 and 427; R. & S., 95, vol. I.; Wurtz, 226, 233; Kem. Th. Chem., 79; Ramsay's Chem. Theory, 80.

CHAPTER XIV.

1.—Synthesis of Water.

When a compound is separated into its constituents and these determined, the compound is said to be **analysed.** Analysis may be of two kinds,—**qualitative,** when the operator simply determines what the constituents are ; **quantitative,** when he goes further and calculates the proportions by weight or volume in which these constituents enter into the compound. The opposite of analysis is **synthesis.** This consists in bringing together the constituents and treating them in such a way that they unite to form the compound required. When water was decomposed by electricity, and it was shown that hydrogen and oxygen composed it, we had a qualitative analysis of water ; on the other hand, when oxygen and hydrogen are caused to unite, and when it is shown that water is the result of the union, we have synthesis of water.

———

2.

EXPERIMENTS.

1. Take a graduated tube called a eudiometer, fill it with mercury, and invert it over mercury in a soup-plate or saucer. Then pass into it a known volume of oxygen and twice the volume of hydrogen, measuring both at the same temperature and pressure. Pass a spark from a Leyden jar, or from a Ruhmkorff's coil, through the mixed gases, Figure 17. Before igniting the gases, press the eudiometer firmly on a rubber pad placed at the

bottom of the plate or saucer. After ignition examine the top of the eudiometer with a good lens.

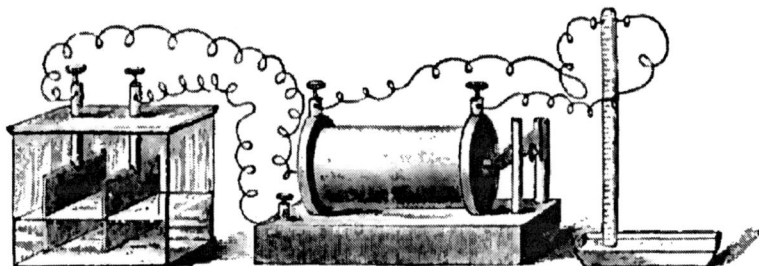

FIG. 17.

2. Repeat this experiment, using equal volumes of the two gases. Test any gas that remains.

3. Try the experiment again, using twice as much oxygen as hydrogen. Test as before any gas that remains.

4. Would it be possible to burn 2 litres of hydrogen in 2 litres of oxygen? Could the process be reversed and 2 litres of oxygen burned in 2 litres of hydrogen? What gas, and what volume of it, would be left in each case?

5.—Composition, by Volume, of Steam.

We have now to find out how many volumes of steam will be produced by the union of two volumes of hydrogen and one of oxygen.

EXPERIMENT.

Fill a eudiometer one-third full of a mixture of hydrogen and oxygen gases—using two volumes of the former to one of the latter. Cover the eudiometer with a large tube, into the top and bottom of which pass tightly-fitting corks perforated with tubes, admitting steam at the top and giving exit to it at the bottom, Fig. 18. The wires from the battery to the eudiometer should pass into the jacket through its upper cork. After the steam has been admitted, mark the height of the mercury above that in the trough, and also the volume of the contained gases, then explode them. After explosion depress the eudiometer, until the mercury in the tube stands the same height above that in the trough as before. Then measure the volume of the water-gas (steam) in the eudiometer, and compare this volume with that of the original mixture.

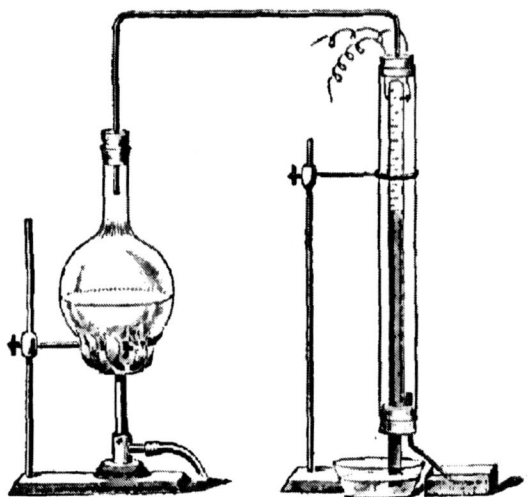

FIG. 18.

If we represent equal volumes of oxygen and of hydrogen by equal squares, and then place in these squares the first letter of the name of these elements, we can represent to the eye, by another figure, the volume of water-gas or steam formed, and the diminution in volume which occurs after union. Thus:

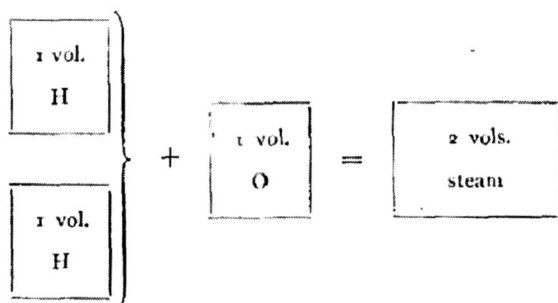

$$\left. \begin{array}{c} \boxed{\begin{array}{c} \text{1 vol.} \\ \text{H} \end{array}} \\ \boxed{\begin{array}{c} \text{1 vol.} \\ \text{H} \end{array}} \end{array} \right\} + \boxed{\begin{array}{c} \text{1 vol.} \\ \text{O} \end{array}} = \boxed{\begin{array}{c} \text{2 vols.} \\ \text{steam} \end{array}}$$

How would you account for the change of volume?

CHAPTER XV.

Definite Proportions.

The object of this chapter is to show that chemical action, whether of combination or decomposition, takes place only between definite weights of the constituents.

EXPERIMENTS.

1. Into a hard glass tube, A, Fig. 19, introduce a weighed quantity of copper oxide. About one gram is a convenient portion to work with. Pass a jet of dry hydrogen through this tube and after all air is expelled heat the tube and contained oxide to redness. Find the weight of the remaining copper. From the result of your work calculate the weight of oxygen that unites with 63·5 parts, by weight of copper.

2. Alter the last experiment by heating the copper that was left in the tube, in a current of air, and find the weight of the black substance (copper oxide) that is formed. Calculate how many parts of oxygen unite with 63·5 parts of copper.

Note.—The student must not expect an absolutely correct result in quantitative work of this kind. The following notes of an actual experiment indicate such a degree of correctness as may be looked for. The true result is to be found in the average of many experiments. For this reason the teacher should keep a record of the best results from year to year.

Weight of empty tube, 19·0045 grams.
Weight of tube with copper oxide in it, 20·005 grams.
Weight of copper oxide, 1·0005 grams.
After heating in current of hydrogen, weight of tube and contents, 19·802, grams.
Loss of weight, ·203 grams; weight of copper, ·7975 grams.

From this it follows that the weight of oxygen that combines with 63·5 parts of copper is 16·17.

3. Vary Ex. 1 by passing the hydrogen through a drying tube filled with lumps of caustic potash before it enters the combustion tube, then passing the escaping gas with the results of the combustion through another drying tube, also filled with pieces of caustic potash. This latter tube must be carefully weighed both before the experiment begins and after it is completed. This will give the weight of the water formed, and from it the weight of hydrogen that unites with 16 parts of oxygen may be found.

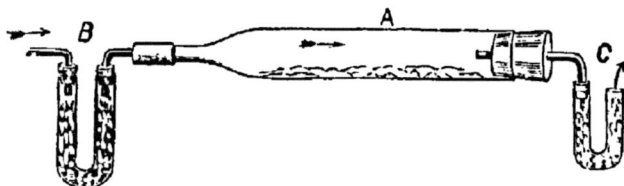

FIG. 19.

4. Heat in a hard glass tube, closed at one end, a weighed quantity of silver nitrate crystals. After all brown fumes cease to come off, find the weight of the resultant solid—pure silver in this case. How many parts of nitrogen trioxide are in union with 108 of silver?

5. Weigh a beaker and a sheet of mica (better, platinum), place on the mica a weighed piece of magnesium wire, invert the beaker over the wire, then heat the mica until all combustion ceases. Weigh again.

6. Close the end of a piece of hard glass tubing about 4 cm. long, and ½ cm. in diameter, A, Fig. 20. Place in this a weighed quantity of red oxide of mercury, then pass the end of this tube into a larger tube B,

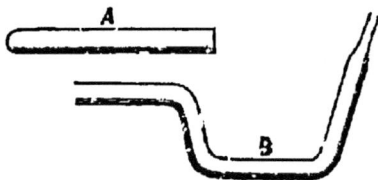

FIG. 20.

and after weighing the whole, heat until the red powder

has all disappeared, weigh again and calculate from your result the proportions in which mercury and oxygen unite in mercuric oxide, HgO.

7. In one beaker prepare some dilute nitric acid, and in another, a solution of potassic hydrate. Pour about 10 cc. of the dilute acid into a graduated measuring glass or tube, add enough of the potash solution to just neutralize this. Observe how much of the latter has been required, then pour the whole into a weighed evaporating dish, evaporate to dryness, but without boiling. Find the weight of the solid substance in the dish. Repeat, at least twice, using different volumes of the acid, and determine if a fixed quantity, by volume, of the acid requires a fixed volume of the alkaline solution to neutralize it, and if it produces relatively an unvarying weight of the salt.

8. Repeat the last experiment, but use hydrochloric acid, and carbonate of sodium.

The results of such experiments as these should show, beyond question, that substances do not take part in chemical actions in random proportions.

These results lead to one of the fundamental laws of chemistry, which is, that each element (or compound radical) unites with other substances in certain fixed and invariable proportions by weight. These proportions are either multiples or sub-multiples of the atomic weight in the case of an element. In the case of a compound, these proportions are either the molecular weight or some simple multiple of it.

One of the chief differences between a solution and a chemical compound is that, in the former, varying quantities of the substances may take part in the action. When a centigram of salt is dissolved in a litre of water the result is just as truly a solution as when 10 grams of the salt are used. Another difference is that solutions, unless agitated artificially, are seldom homogeneous; while chemical combination throughout a mass must be absolutely the same in every part.

See Tilden, 80 ; D. & W., 39 ; R., 14 ; Wurtz, 3 ; R. & S., 63.

CHAPTER XVI.

Some Chemical Calculations.

It has been said in the chapter on symbols and equations (VII), that in any chemical equation the sum of the atomic weights of the elements on one side must equal the sum of those on the other. Some applications of this principle will now be made.

1.

When hydrogen is prepared from zinc and dilute sulphuric acid, the following equation expresses the reaction that takes place :—

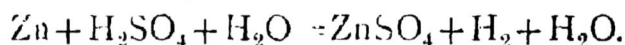

$$Zn + H_2SO_4 + H_2O = ZnSO_4 + H_2 + H_2O.$$

From this we see that 65 parts, by weight, of zinc, 98 of sulphuric acid and 18 of water, yield 161 parts, by weight, of zinc sulphate, 2 of hydrogen and 18 of water. The water evidently takes no part in the chemical action, so far as the evolution of hydrogen is concerned, and so, in our calculation, it may be neglected. We are now ready to work out some numerical problems of which. the following are examples :—

1. Suppose we required 11·2 grams of hydrogen, how much zinc and how much sulphuric acid would be used up in obtaining it?

65 "parts" by weight of zinc and 98 of sulphuric acid yield 2 of hydrogen, then 11·2 "parts" by weight of hydrogen come from $65 \times \frac{11·2}{2}$ of zinc and $98 \times \frac{11·2}{2}$ of sulphuric acid, but a *part* may be any unit of weight whatever, since it i. a general term, and is used as the unit throughout the problem, hence 11·2 grams of hydrogen come from $\frac{65 \times 11·2}{2·0}$ of zinc and $\frac{98 \times 11·2}{2·0}$ of sulphuric acid.

2. Iron filings treated with hydrochloric acid yield hydrogen according to the equation $Fe + 2HCl = FeCl_2 + H_2$.

If 40 grams of iron were used in the experiment, how much pure hydrochloric acid should be taken, and how much hydrogen would be obtained?

Solution :—

56 parts by weight of iron, and 73 of hydrochloric acid yield 127 of chloride of iron and 2 of hydrogen; then 40 of iron would require $\frac{40}{56}$ of 73 parts of acid and would yield $\frac{40}{56} \times 127$ of the chloride, and $\frac{40}{56} \times 2$ of hydrogen.

3. When oxygen is prepared from chlorate of potassium and manganese dioxide the equation is :

$KClO_3 + MnO_2 = KCl + MnO_2 + 3O$, hence 122·6 parts by weight of potassic chlorate, heated with 87 parts of manganese dioxide, yield 87 parts of dioxide, 48 of oxygen and 74·6 parts of chloride of potassium. Here also the dioxide is unchanged and may be neglected. Then x grams of the chlorate will yield $\frac{x}{122.6} \times 48$ grams of oxygen, and x grams of oxygen may be obtained from $\frac{x}{48} \times 122.6$ grams of chlorate.

2.—Questions and Exercises.

1. Five grams of sodium are placed on water, and the hydrogen resulting from the chemical action is collected, afterwards the water is evaporated and the white salt that is obtained is weighed. Theoretically, how much hydrogen and how much of this salt would there be?

2. If 5 grams of potassium had been used in the last question what would then have been the answers?

3. If 5 grams of copper oxide, CuO, were reduced in a current of hydrogen, what products would be obtained and how much of each by weight? How much hydrogen by weight would be required to complete this chemical action?

4. If 10 grams of lead peroxide, PbO_2, are reduced to lead oxide, PbO, how much oxygen would be given off in the operation, and if this oxygen immediately united with hydrogen, how many grams of the compound would be formed?

5. An excess of iron filings is treated with 50 grams of a solution of hydrochloric acid, containing 25% by weight of pure acid, how many grams of hydrogen will be produced, and how many grams of the compound of iron and acid will be formed?

6. If 50 grams of chlorate of potash were entirely decomposed by heat into potassium chloride and oxygen, and the latter collected over water, then if a jet of burning hydrogen were passed into the jar and kept there until all the oxygen was used up, what would be the weight of the resultant compound?

7. 10 grams of water are decomposed by electricity, 10 grams are decomposed by the action of sodium, 10 grams are decomposed by the action of potassium, and 10 grams are converted into steam and passed over red hot iron filings. How much hydrogen would be obtained in each case?

CHAPTER XVII.

Combustion.

It has been customary to classify bodies as combustible or as supporters of combustion. The object of this chapter is to show that there is no such division of substances; that combustion is a chemical action in which at least two substances are equally concerned, and that the phenomena of combustion are produced by the energy with which the chemical union goes on.

1.

When two substances enter into chemical union, or act upon each other chemically in any way, the action is usually accompanied by change of temperature, change of volume, or by both these phenomena. When the combination of two substances is accompanied by light and heat (the light as a consequence of the heat) there is said to be either *glowing* or *combustion*—glowing, if a mass of solid matter simply becomes red hot—combustion, either if a flame is produced, as in the case of any burning gas, or if the solid, while glowing, gradually changes into an incandescent gaseous compound, as in the case of charcoal.

Burning or *combustion* is generally caused by some substance uniting with oxygen, hence the popular assertion that oxygen is a supporter of combustion. Examples of this may be found in the experiments under oxygen. As some of the following experiments will show, however, oxygen is not necessary for combustion.

———

2.

EXPERIMENTS.

1. In Fig. 21, A is a glass tube about 3 or 4 centimetres in diameter, drawn to about half that diameter at

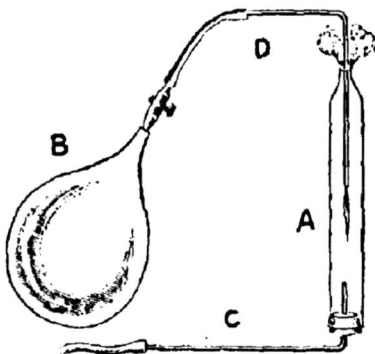

FIG. 21.

the upper end and closed with a perforated stopper at the lower end ; C leads either to an ordinary gas cock or to a gas holder. After the air is expelled from A, fire the escaping gas at the top. B is a gas bag, or gas holder, filled with oxygen, and the delivery tube D is gradually lowered until the nozzle passes into the interior of A, at the same time the oxygen is being driven out of B by pressure. The gas that escapes through D ought to take fire at the top of A just as the tube D is lowered through the mouth of A, and continue to burn in the interior. Try the experiment using both coal gas and hydrogen passing through C, and both oxygen and air passing through D. Next, reverse the operation.

2. Heat some sulphur in a test-tube, until the tube becomes filled with the vapour, then lower into it some copper foil or a braid of very fine copper wire.

3. Fit up an apparatus, as in Fig. 40; put into the flask equal portions of common salt (sodium chloride) and manganese dioxide, then pour on this some sulphuric acid and gently heat the whole. Soon a greenish yellow gas will come off which will collect in the jar at the right. This gas is chlorine. As soon as the jar is full of the gas, as may be seen by the colour, drop into it some powdered antimony or arsenic.

4. Prepare another jar of chlorine and lower into it a et of burning hydrogen.

5. Use the apparatus, Fig. 21, but cause a jet of chlorine o pass through D, and hydrogen through C.

These experiments are sufficient to show that "combustible" and "supporter of combustion" hardly express ie relations between the pairs of substances which here nter into combination with each other. A better way) state the case would be, that two kinds of matter which :t on each other as do oxygen and hydrogen, or hydro-:n and chlorine are *mutually* combustible; or that if ere are two gases, A and B, of which A burns in pre-nce of B, it is equally true that B burns in presence A.

3.—Questions.

1. When coal is heated to a certain degree it unites with part of the air. In this case should we say that the coal burns, the air burns, or they both burn?

2. Air burns in coal gas, coal gas burns in air, which is the supporter of combustion?

CHAPTER XVIII.

1.—Is Air an Element, a Compound, or a Mixture of Gases?

It has been learned that water, one of the substances of most common occurrence, is a compound of two gases. We are now in a position to study another very common substance—the air. The first step will be to determine, if possible, whether it is an element, a compound, or a mixture of two or more gases.

Experiments.

1. Cover a cork, about two inches in diameter, with a piece of tin and float on a soup-plate full of water.

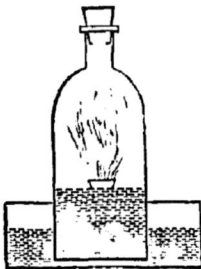
Fig. 23.

Take a piece of phosphorus about the size of a pea, and place it on the cork. Now set fire to the phosphorus, and then cover it quickly with a beaker or small bell jar, placed mouth downwards, as in Fig. 23. Allow it to stand thus for 15 or 20 minutes.

After the white fumes have entirely disappeared, lower the plate and jar into water until the water stands at the same height on the inside and the outside of the jar; then test the gas by (a) passing a lighted splinter into it, (b) passing a little of it through lime water, (c) driving some of it into a test-tube inverted over mercury, then passing pyrogallate of potash into this tube. In the last case, observe if a material darkening of the liquid takes place after it enters the tube, or if there is any considerable decrease in the volume of the gas.

2. Invert a test-tube of air over mercury and pass into it some pyrogallate of potash to the depth of a couple of centimetres.

3. Wet the inside of a bell jar with water, and drop into it some fine iron filings. Then shake the jar so that the inside may become closely sprinkled with the filings. Place the jar, mouth downward, over a soup-plate filled with water, and allow the whole to stand for a day or two. Carefully invert the jar by slipping the hand under its mouth, and as it is turned mouth upward, allow the water in it to run to the bottom; thus an influx of air is prevented. Test the gas in the jar with a burning splinter.

2. Questions.

1. Pyrogallate of potash turns brown in the atmosphere and takes part of it up. What is the inference?

2. Is air a mixture of at least two substances, a chemical compound of two substances, or a single element? What reasons have you for your answer?

Explanation.—The gas that was left in the jar after the phosphorus burned, and the fumes were absorbed, was almost entirely nitrogen.

6

3.—Volumetric Composition of the Atmosphere.

The quantities, by volume, in which oxygen and nitrogen are mixed in the atmosphere may be determined in two ways,—(1) by causing the oxygen to unite with some substance to form an oxide which may be got rid of by solution ; (2) by causing the oxygen to unite with hydrogen to form steam, whose volume when condensed to water may be neglected in the calculation.

EXPERIMENT.

Burn a piece of phosphorus as in experiment 1 of section 1, but do not allow bubbles of gas to escape, and after all white fumes have disappeared measure the condensation which the gas in the jar has undergone. This may be done by marking the level of the water *in* the jar just when the combustion of the phosphorus is completed ; then after all oxide is dissolved depress the jar in a tank until the water stands at the same level inside and outside of it ; again mark the height of the water. Now invert the jar, fill it with water and measure the contents in a graduated glass. Measure also the volume between the marks and compare this volume with the volume of the whole jar.

4.—Additional Exercises.

1. Try if a jet of burning hydrogen will continue to burn when plunged into nitrogen. Reverse the process and try if a jet of nitrogen will burn in hydrogen.

2. Will nitrogen burn in oxygen, or oxygen burn in nitrogen?

3. Is there any free phosphorus left on the tin after combustion has ceased in experiment 1, sec. 1? Would the use of a larger

quantity of phosphorus cause any variation in the volume of gas
remaining after chemical action has ceased?

4. Take a graduated tube about 30 centimetres long and 3 centimetres wide, closed at one end by a stop-
cock, or by a piece of rubber tube and
a pinchcock.   Invert it over a vessel
9 or 10 centimetres in depth, filled with
water.   Fix the tube in a support, taking
care that the water stands at the same
level on the inside as it does on the outside of the tube.   Then pass up to the
top of the tube a piece of phosphorus
attached to a copper wire, as in Fig. 24.
To attach the wire to the phosphorus, fuse
it under water in a test-tube, introduce
the end of the wire into it, and then let it
cool. Leave the whole twenty-four hours,
then withdraw the phosphorus and adjust
the level of the water inside and outside
the tube ; read off the volume of the gas
remaining in the graduated tube.   The

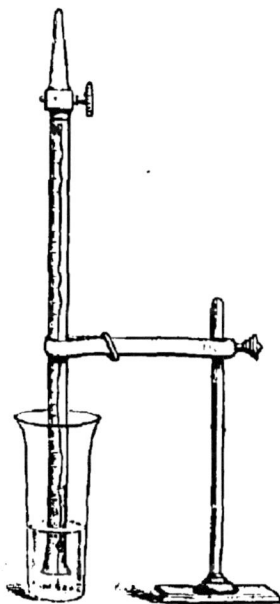

Fig. 24.

volume of gas at the beginning and at the end of the experiment
must be reduced to that at standard temperature and pressure.

5. Pass into a eudiometer over mercury a measured volume of air,
dried by passing it over lumps of calcium chloride in a tube, then
pass in half as much dried hydrogen, and explode the mixture.
Note reduction in volume of the gases.

Explanation.—It has been learned before that hydrogen and oxygen unite in the proportion by volume of 2
to 1, hence one-third of the reduction of the volume of
the mixed gases is due to the oxygen of the air uniting
with the hydrogen.   From careful determinations made
in this way, oxygen has been found to form 21% by
volume of the air, and nitrogen 79%.   By weight, the

IMAGE EVALUATION
TEST TARGET (MT-3)

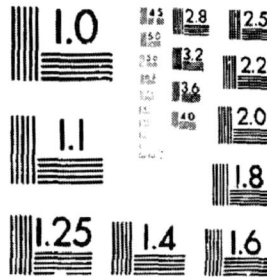

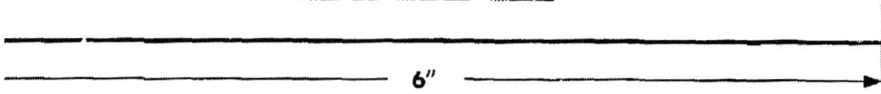

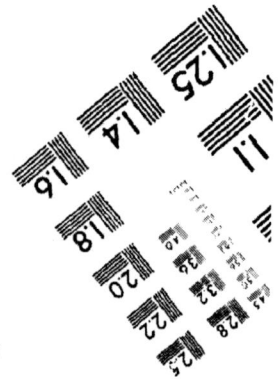

6"

Photographic
Sciences
Corporation

23 WEST MAIN STREET
WEBSTER, N.Y. 14580
(716) 872-4503

percentage is somewhat different. In terms of volumes of hydrogen, we have

21 vols. of oxygen become by weight $21 \times 16 =$ 336
79 " nitrogen " " $79 \times 14 =$ 1106

$$\overline{\qquad\qquad 1442}$$

That is $\frac{336}{1442}$ of the whole is oxygen, $= 23 \cdot 3\%$.

In addition to the experimental reasons given in this chapter for considering air to be a mixture, the following are further proofs of the same fact :—

(1) A mixture of oxygen and nitrogen may be made which cannot be distinguished from air, either chemically or physically.

(2) The gases are not present in the proportions corresponding to their atomic weights, or in simple multiples of their atomic weights, yet they could not be present in other proportions if air were a compound.

(3) Air is soluble in water, and if the air dissolved in water be expelled by heating or by the air pump, and the gases collected, the oxygen and nitrogen are found not in the same proportion in which they were before solution ; more of the latter gas in proportion is given off from the solution ; this, of course, would be impossible in the case of a compound.

(4) Air that has been collected at different places gives, on analysis, slightly different proportions by weight.

CHAPTER XIX.

1.---Nitrogen---Its Properties and Preparation.

EXPERIMENTS.

1. The simplest method of obtaining nitrogen is by burning phosphorus, or some other combustible which will form a readily soluble oxide, in a bell jar over water. The student should repeat the first experiment of the previous chapter. After the white fumes have been absorbed, depress the jar in a trough of water until the level of the water inside is the same as that outside. Then remove the cork and test the gas that remains with litmus paper, with a glowing splinter, and with a jet of burning hydrogen.

2. Prepare a hydrogen apparatus with a delivery tube as shown in Fig. 25. After the hydrogen is burning freely at the mouth of the tube invert a gas cylinder over it so that the mouth of the cylinder will be under water in the dish. Watch closely what occurs. The instant the flame goes out disconnect the delivery tube from the flask. After the water

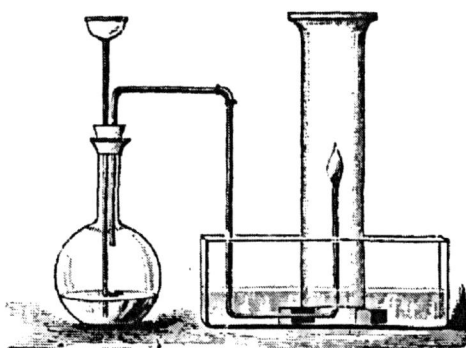

FIG. 25.

has ceased to rise in the cylinder slip a glass cover under it and turn it mouth upwards, but do not let the water run out, else air will become mixed with the gas in the cylinder. Test this gas as in the previous experiment.

Tabulate the properties and appearance of nitrogen, oxygen, hydrogen, and air.

2.—Additional Exercises.

1. The apparatus represented in Figure 26 may be used for preparing nitrogen by passing air over red-hot copper. A is a U tube filled with calcic chloride, B is a straight tube filled with fine, bright copper filings, and C is a large-mouthed bottle used as a gas holder, one of its tubes passing through the cork, the other passing to the bottom of the bottle; D is a piece of rubber tubing attached to the latter of these tubes in order to convert it into a

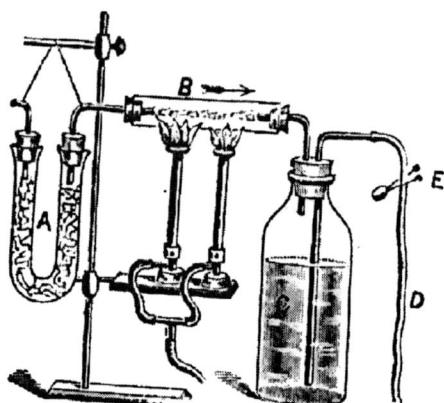

FIG. 26.

syphon, and draw off the water from the bottle. E is a spring clip which may be kept slightly open by putting a small wedge in it. On starting the experiment, the bottle must be full of water. When the copper has been made red-hot, the syphon must be made to act *very slowly* by regulating the clip, and as the water flows out of the bottle, air is drawn through the U tube and passes over the red-hot copper. The nitrogen is collected in the bottle. At what stage in this experiment would air begin to pass out of the tube?

2. Heat some potassic nitrate in a tube or crucible until it gives readily an alkaline reaction. It has then changed into the nitrite.* Mix this salt with ammonium chloride, heat them in a test-tube and collect over water the gas given off.

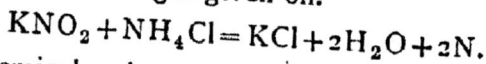

$$KNO_2 + NH_4Cl = KCl + 2H_2O + 2N.$$

Explain the chemical actions involved and classify them.

---

* The alkalinity is due to the nitrite beginning to undergo a further decomposition, by which the oxide of potassium is formed, and it is a strong alkali.

3.—Notes on Nitrogen.

Nitrogen: symbol N.; atomic weight, 14; molecular weight, 28; molecular volume, 2.

On account of its chemical inertness, nitrogen forms many unstable compounds, and of these a large number are liable to sudden and often very violent decomposition : for example, nitro-glycerine, and chloride of nitrogen.

Nitrogen occurs free in the air, of which it forms by volume 79%, and by weight 77% ; it is also a constituent of almost all organic substances, and enters into the composition of a large number of inorganic compounds. It serves to dilute the oxygen in the atmosphere, but takes no direct part in the support of animal life. It is doubtful if it acts directly in support of vegetable life, neither does it enter into direct chemical combinations except very rarely and by special treatment.

CHAPTER XX.

Compounds of Nitrogen and Oxygen.

Nitrogen and oxygen do not unite directly to form compounds as do hydrogen and oxygen ; there are. however, five oxides of nitrogen known, all of them being obtained by the decomposition of other compounds,

These oxides are :

Nitrous oxide or nitrogen monoxide	N_2O,
Nitric " " dioxide	NO,
Nitrogen trioxide	N_2O_3.
Nitrogen peroxide or nitrogen tetroxide	NO_2,
Nitrogen pentoxide	N_2O_5.

§ 1.—Nitrous Oxide

EXPERIMENTS.

1. Put 25 grams of commercial ammonic nitrate, NH_4NO_3, into an oxygen generating apparatus, connected with three bottles, as in Fig. 27. The first bottle should contain a solution of ferrous sulphate, the second

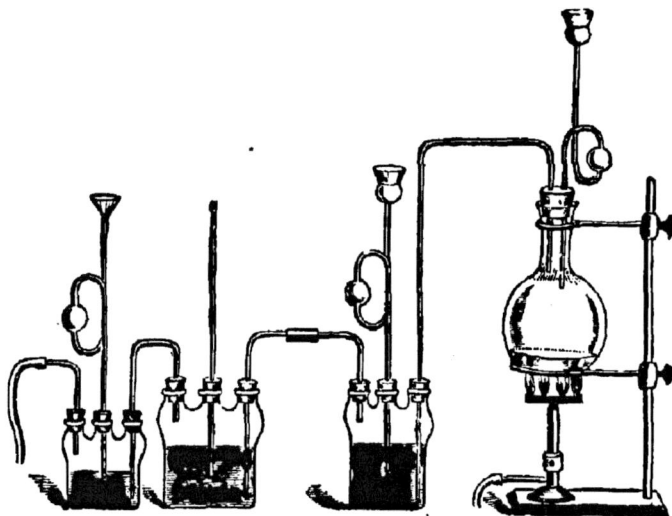

FIG. 27.

a solution of caustic potash, and the third, water. Heat the nitrate gently, and nitrogen monoxide will be given off. Thus prepared, the gas will be found mixed with nitrogen dioxide and chlorine gas. The first will be removed by passing through the ferrous sulphate solution, and the second by passing through the caustic potash solution.

If the nitrate be chemically pure, the wash bottles may be omitted. The reaction may be thus represented:

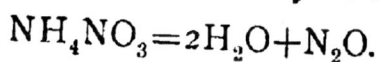

$$NH_4NO_3 = 2H_2O + N_2O.$$

2. Collect several jars of the gas over warm water and perform the following experiments:—

(a). Plunge a lighted taper into the first jar; also test it with a glowing splinter, as in the case of oxygen.

(b). Burn a piece of phosphorus, carbon or sulphur in another of the jars.

(c). Explode a mixture of the gas with hydrogen.

(d). Place another jar, mouth downward, over *cold* water, and then shake. Let it stand for 24 hours. Vary this experiment by filling a 4 or 5 inch test-tube with the gas, put a little water in it, close the mouth tightly by putting the thumb over it, then shake the water up with the gas, invert the tube, dip the mouth under water and remove the thumb. Test the water that rose in the tube with litmus.

3. Try the effect of dry nitrous oxide upon litmus.

4. How could you distinguish nitrous oxide from oxygen?

5. Using the apparatus of Fig. 25, burn a jet of hydrogen in nitrous oxide. What are the substances formed? Write equation. What change in volume, if any, takes place during the combustion? Explain.

6. Try if a mixture of hydrogen and nitrous oxide will explode when an electric spark is passed through it.

2.—Notes on Nitrous Oxide.

Nitrous Oxide: formula, N_2O *; molecular weight, 44 ; vapour density, 22.*

"Laughing gas" is an old name for this compound. It derives this name from the fact that many persons after inhaling a mixture of the gas and air are compelled to laugh—*nolens volens.* On inhaling more of the gas temporary unconsciousness is produced ; it is therefore frequently used as an anæsthetic for minor operations in surgery.

Nitrous oxide is soluble in cold water to the extent of 130 per cent of its own volume ; it may be condensed to a liquid by a cold of $0°$ C, and a pressure of 30 atmospheres. Liquid nitrous oxide when mixed with carbon disulphide, CS_2, forms a freezing mixture capable of producing a cold of—$140°$ C.

3.—Nitric Oxide or Nitrogen Dioxide.

EXPERIMENTS.

1. Place some copper filings in a hydrogen generating apparatus similar to that in Fig. 7, add some warm water, and then pour down the funnel tube some strong nitric acid. The gas that first forms should be allowed to escape. The reaction may be thus represented :—

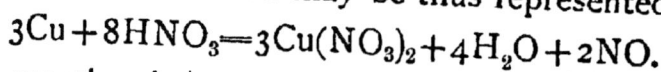

$$3Cu + 8HNO_3 = 3Cu(NO_3)_2 + 4H_2O + 2NO.$$

The reaction here represented is really the result of two separate and successive ones, thus :—

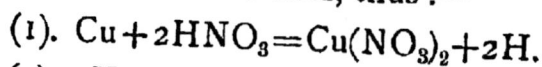

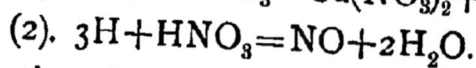

(1). $Cu + 2HNO_3 = Cu(NO_3)_2 + 2H.$

(2). $3H + HNO_3 = NO + 2H_2O.$

The explanation of this will be found in chap. XXI, sect. 5.

Collect, over water, two bell jars and two large test-tubes full of the gas.

2. Place one of the tubes that is full of gas, mouth downwards, over a small quantity of water in a dish, then pass air, a little at a time, into the tube.* Test the water with litmus both before the air is passed in, then again after the brown fumes have disappeared.

Unless the operator is careful in this experiment a wrong result will be obtained. When the jar is filled with the gas it should be removed to a clean plate with a little water on it, so that the gas will be tested and not a solution of the brown fumes formed by bubbles of it coming in contact with air.

3. Test the gas in one of the bell jars with a glowing splinter, a blazing splinter, a burning taper, a piece of slightly-ignited phosphorus, a piece of brightly-burning phosphorus.

4. Lift one of the test-tubes full of the gas and place it, mouth downwards, in a vessel containing a cold solution of copperas (ferrous sulphate), $FeSO_4$.

Vary this experiment as follows :—

Pour some well-cooled solution of ferrous sulphate, $FeSO_4$, into a beaker full of the gas ; then hold the hand over the beaker's mouth and shake vigorously. Note the two phenomena that occur.

---

* The air may readily be driven into the tube by using an empty flask fitted up like the one in figure 25. When water is poured down the funnel, air is forced out through the delivery tube.

4.—Notes on Nitric Oxide.

Nitric oxide: formula, NO; molecular weight, 30; vapour density, 15.

Nitric oxide condenses to a liquid at—11°C. and a pressure of 104 atmospheres. It does not unite with water to form an acid. One test for this gas is its reaction with air or free oxygen; another is that with a solution of ferrous sulphate a dark ring or layer is formed on the liquid, as seen in ex. 4, in the preceding section.

———

5.—Composition by Volume of Nitrous Oxide and Nitric Oxide.

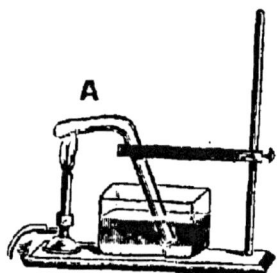
Fig. 28.

Prepare a hard glass tube, bent as A in the Fig. 28. Fill this with washed nitrous oxide gas, having previously dropped into the tube a piece of sodium, or of potassium, about as large as a pea. Dip the mouth of the tube, when filled with gas, under mercury, and by jarring it, get the sodium into a position just below A. Then heat it strongly. The hot sodium decomposes the nitrous oxide to form oxide of sodium and the nitrogen is left. The volume of the nitrogen should be the same as that of the original gas.

Nitric oxide may be decomposed in the same way, but the volume of nitrogen in this case is only one-half that of the oxide taken.

6.—Questions and Exercises.

1. Pass nitrogen into nitric oxide.

2. Is it the air as a whole, or one of the constituents of it, that causes the brown coloured gas to appear with nitric oxide?

3. What reasons have you for believing that nitric oxide does not burn?

4. Will dry nitric oxide change litmus?

5. Pass oxygen into a jar of nitric oxide over water very slowly so that the brown fumes may disappear as rapidly as formed. Account for the result obtained.

6. When air was passed into a jar of nitric oxide over water until brown fumes ceased to appear and be dissolved, what remained? Apply tests to find out if your conclusion is a correct one. Was the result different when oxygen was passed in?

7.—Nitrogen Trioxide.

EXPERIMENT.

Fit a Florence flask with a cork and delivery tube, and place on a retort stand, as in Fig. 29. To the delivery tube attach a U tube, immersed in a freezing mixture of salt and snow. Connect the other end of the U tube with a glass

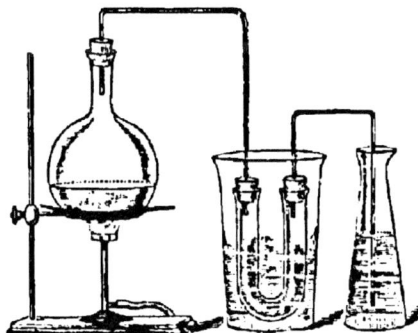

FIG. 29.

tube leading to a vessel containing ice-water. Place 10 grams of starch in the flask and cover with nitric acid. Gently heat the generating flask and nitrogen trioxide will be plentifully produced, part of it being condensed in the U tube, and the remainder passing on into the ice-water.

Instead of starch, white arsenic, A$_2$O$_3$, may be used. The reaction in this case may be thus represented :

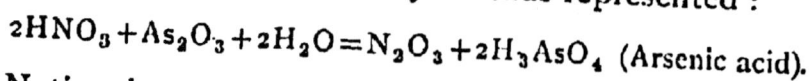

$$2HNO_3 + As_2O_3 + 2H_2O = N_2O_3 + 2H_3AsO_4 \text{ (Arsenic acid).}$$

Notice the colour of the gas. It is condensed to a liquid by a temperature of—18° C. Try to collect some of the gas over water. Has it any smell?

The gas, as condensed in the U tube, is green in colour. This is owing to nitrogen peroxide being mixed with it. If the generating flask be disconnected and a current of nitric oxide passed through the U tube, the brown gas that passes off, if again condensed, will be indigo blue in colour; this will be pure nitrogen trioxide.

By using for a condenser a piece of thick glass tubing drawn out, as shown in Fig. 30, the liquid may be preserved ; for by using a blowpipe flame the tube may readily be sealed at A and B ; and internal pressure will then prevent the fluid from evaporating. The tube must be strong enough, however, to withstand the pressure.

Fig. 30.

7.—Nitrogen Tetroxide or Nitrogen Peroxide.

This gas is prepared by heating lead nitrate and condensing the gas, as in the case of the trioxide. It is the substance most largely formed when nitric oxide comes in contact with air. In the preparation, trioxide and tetroxide are mixed, but the former may be changed into the latter by a current of oxygen. The liquid peroxide is yellowish or brownish in colour. This substance has the formula NO_2 and is introduced here because of theoretical considerations.

There is still another oxide of nitrogen, viz., the pentoxide, N_2O_5, but as it is difficult of preparation and of no practical value its study may be omitted.

Fill out the following schedule:—

	APPEARANCE.	SOLUBILITY IN WATER.	ACIDITY OF HYDRATES.	PHYSICAL STATE AT 0°.
N_2O				
$N O$........				
N_2O_3				
$N O_2$........				

8.—Law of Multiple Proportions.

These oxides of nitrogen illustrate the Law of **Multiple Proportions** in chemistry. Beginning with the lowest oxide and going to the highest, there are successively one, two, three, four and five volumes of oxygen united with two volumes of nitrogen. Expressed in another way, the quantity of oxygen, which is the variable element here, is an integral multiple in every case, both of unit volume and of atomic weight. The relative quantities of oxygen are in the ratio of the numbers 1, 2, 3, 4 and 5, and these are the only proportions in which the elements can be made to unite.

CHAPTER XXI.

1.—Acids of Nitrogen.

Nitrogen, in union with hydrogen and oxygen, forms two well defined acids that have the formula HNO_2 and HNO_3, and are named *nitrous and nitric* acids respectively. Some salts corresponding to a third acid, *hyponitrous*, are known, but the acid itself has not been isolated ; and, as its salts are somewhat rare and of little value in elementary work, it will be passed over with the remark that, if separated, its formula would be HNO, and that its salts have the composition MNO when M is a monad base.

2.—Nitrous Acid.

EXPERIMENTS.

1. Pass nitrogen trioxide into cold water and test for acid properties.

Definition.—An oxide which unites chemically with the water, and thus forms an acid, is called an **anhydride.**

2. Pass nitrogen trioxide into a solution of potassic hydrate until it is neutral, then evaporate ; the salt obtained is *potassic nitrite.*

3. Add a few drops of nitrous acid to a solution of potassium permanganate.

3.—Questions and Exercises.

1. Nitrous acid is an unstable compound decomposing, upon standing, into nitric acid, nitric oxide, and water, thus :—

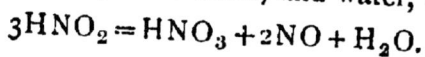

$$3HNO_2 = HNO_3 + 2NO + H_2O.$$

This may be shown by filling a bottle with nitrous oxide within an inch of the top, tightly corking it and letting it stand for a couple of days. On removing the cork, brown fumes are formed. After standing for some time longer, it will answer to the test for nitric acid.

2. Potassium permanganate is very readily broken up by substances that absorb oxygen. How can you account for the result observed in experiment 3, sec. 2?

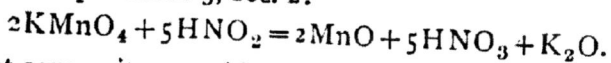

$$2KMnO_4 + 5HNO_2 = 2MnO + 5HNO_3 + K_2O.$$

3. Heat some nitrous acid solution, then test the residue for nitric acid.

4. Water tainted with sewage always contains nitrites and nitrates in solution. The common test for this is to pour some of the water into a weak solution of permanganate of potash and watch for decoloration. How do you explain this chemically?

5. When nitrites are acidulated with acetic acid they give a white precipitate with nitrate of silver. Nitrites are soluble in water. Try nitrite of potash, as prepared in ex. 2, sec. 2, for these reactions.

4.—Nitric Acid.

EXPERIMENTS.

1. Put into a tubulated glass retort 30 grams of powdered nitrate of potash, KNO_3, and an equal weight of strong sulphuric acid, H_2SO_4. Place the end of the retort in a flask which is made to float on a basin of water as in Fig. 31. Apply heat to the retort. Soon a yellowish colored liquid distils over and is collected in the cool flask. The reaction may be

Fig. 31.

represented as taking place in two successive stages, the

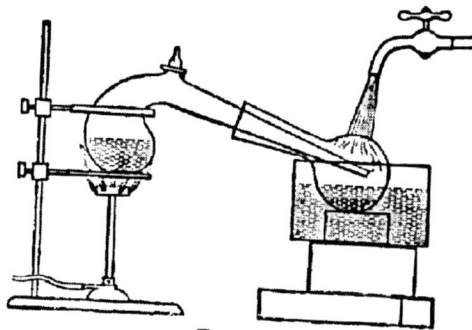

7

first requiring a comparatively low, the second a high, temperature.

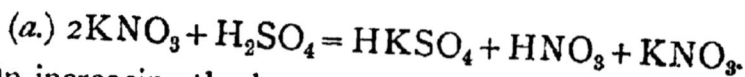

(*a.*) $2KNO_3 + H_2SO_4 = HKSO_4 + HNO_3 + KNO_3.$

On increasing the heat more acid comes off, the second reaction being represented as follows :—

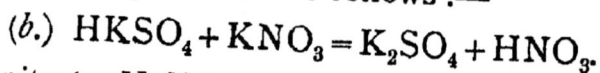

(*b.*) $HKSO_4 + KNO_3 = K_2SO_4 + HNO_3.$

Sodic nitrate, $NaNO_3$, may be used instead of potassic nitrate in the preparation of nitric acid; in fact sodic nitrate is generally used when this acid is to be manufactured on a large scale.

2. Heat a few drops of the acid until nearly boiling, then hold close to its surface a piece of glowing charcoal. Vary this by heating strongly some fine charcoal dust, then dropping on it some strong nitric acid.

3. Warm a few drops of the acid in a small evaporating dish, then drop into it a bit of phosphorus.

4. Immerse some undyed wool, silk or other organic substance in a little of the acid.

5. Add a few drops of the acid to a solution of indigo.

6. Place some copper filings in the bottom of a test-tube, and then pour in some of the acid. When all action has ceased, evaporate to dryness the solution which has been formed.

————

5.—Notes on Nitric Acid.

The anhydride of nitric acid is nitrogen pentoxide, N_2O_5.

Nitric acid is said to be a powerful *oxidizing agent*, that is, it readily yields its oxygen to substances which have an affinity for that element. This oxygen, at the moment of its liberation from the acid, is said to be in its *nascent* state.

$$2HNO_3 = H_2O + 2NO_2 + O.$$

Nitric acid is a strong monobasic acid. When metals act on it, nitrates are formed by the replacement of the hydrogen by the metal, but the nascent hydrogen at once acts on part of the nitric acid present, forming with it, according to accompanying circumstances, nitrous acid or one of the oxides of nitrogen, or sometimes even reducing it to ammonia.

The brown fumes that arise when nitric acid is being prepared are caused by its partial decomposition; this occurs at the boiling point of the acid, about 68° C. Similar fumes are always present over *very strong* nitric acid contained in a glass-stoppered bottle.

In preparing the acid, hydro-potassic sulphate, $KHSO_4$, the acid salt, is first formed; but at a high temperature the further reaction resulting in the formation of the neutral potassic sulphate, K_2SO_4, takes place. The heat necessary for this causes the decomposition of the acid formed, however.

6.—Tests.

1. Nitric acid heated with copper filings gives off brown fumes of N_2O_3 and NO_2.

2. Dissolve a few crystals of ferrous sulphate, $FeSO_4$, in water in a test-tube. Add a few drops of sulphuric acid and allow the whole to cool. Then turn the test-tube sideways and gently pour nitric acid, or a nitrate in

solution, down its side.   The phenomenon which results will always enable us to recognize nitric acid or a nitrate.*

3. Nitric acid bleaches indigo solution.

7.—Questions and Exercises.

1. Zinc treated with dilute sulphuric acid gives hydrogen.   What is produced when nitric acid is substituted for sulphuric?

2. $C + 2HNO_3 =$

   $4P + 10HNO_3 =$

Complete these equations.

3. Nitric acid acts on copper and forms the salt cupric nitrate $Cu(NO_3)_2$; find out whether it acts similarly on other common metals such as lead, zinc, iron and mercury.

4. The principle of atomicity is employed in writing the formulas of salts from nitric acid by replacing one atom of the hydrogen of the acid with one atom of a monad metal; two atoms of the hydrogen of the acid in two molecules, with one atom of a diad metal, and so on.   For example :

Acid.	Salt.	Name of Salt.
HNO_3	$AgNO_3$	Silver Nitrate.
$2HNO_3$	$Cu(NO_3)_2$	Copper Nitrate.
$3HNO_3$	$Bi(NO_3)_3$	Bismuth Nitrate.

In the same way symbolize the salts which nitric acid may form with the following metals : Potassium, calcium, lead.

5. Explain the action of nitric acid on a solution of sulphate of indigo.

6. Twenty grams of sodic nitrate are heated with an excess of sulphuric acid, assuming that the acid sulphate of sodium alone is

---

*Another method of performing this experiment is to drop a little nitric acid or a solution of a nitrate into a porcelain evaporating dish, add a little sulphuric acid, then set the dish on ice or in cold water until cool.   After it has cooled, drop into it some solution of ferrous sulphate.   If a precipitate is thrown down by the sulphuric acid, filter and test the filtrate.

formed, and that the acid produced is led into a solution of potassic hydroxide, what salt would be formed, and how much of it? Write equations for the reactions.

8.—Nitrates.

EXPERIMENTS.

1. Test as many nitrates as you can find for solubility.

2. Heat different nitrates, and test them by the ordinary method to ascertain whether oxygen is given off; then sprinkle on them some powdered charcoal, also some sulphur. Do all the nitrates give off brown fumes when heated?

9.—Notes on Nitrates.

All nitrates are soluble, and yield oxygen when heated, thus,—$KNO_3 = KNO_2 + O$.

To this ammonium nitrate, NH_4NO_3, seems to be an exception, probably on account of being composed of two unstable radicals. When gently heated it yields, as we have seen, $N_2O + 2H_2O$; but when strongly heated breaks up into water, oxygen and free nitrogen, the oxygen being first given off, thus:

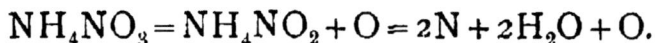

$$NH_4NO_3 = NH_4NO_2 + O = 2N + 2H_2O + O.$$

The nitrates of the metallic bases, when heated, form the oxide of the metal, free oxygen and nitrogen peroxide, thus:

$$Pb(NO_3)_2 = PbO + 2NO_2 + O.$$

Those of the alkaline bases lose oxygen on heating, become first reduced to nitrites and finally to the oxides of the metals.

A substance supposed to be a nitrate may be tested by treating it with sulphuric acid, which frees the nitric acid, the latter may then be tested for, as in sec. 6.

10.—Additional Exercises.

1. In the test for nitric acid by the use of ferrous sulphate, the brown layer is due to the formation of nitric oxide with ferric sulphate. Compare Ex. 4, Sec. 3, Chap. xx :

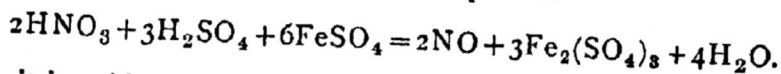

$$2HNO_3 + 3H_2SO_4 + 6FeSO_4 = 2NO + 3Fe_2(SO_4)_3 + 4H_2O.$$

If nitric oxide be prepared and passed (1) into warm solution of ferrous sulphate, (2) into cold solution, the brown ring will be found in the latter case only, thus showing that the oxide is soluble in warm sulphate solution.

2. Investigate some of the properties of potassic nitrite by (a) throwing some of it upon red-hot charcoal, (b) by placing a drop of any strong acid upon it.

3. Boil some starch in water so as to form a paste. Then add some iodide of potassium solution, and allow the whole to cool. The reaction, which occurs on adding free nitrous acid to the mixture, forms, when taken in connection with the nitrate of silver test, a sure indication of the presence of nitrous acid.

4. Put into a test-tube a little strong nitric acid, then plug the mouth of the tube with horsehair or fine wood shavings, and heat the acid to boiling.

5. Dissolve some common salt (sodium chloride), also some silver nitrate, mix the solutions, filter and evaporate the filtrate, test the result and see if it is a nitrate. The white precipitate was silver chloride. Why did it appear as a precipitate, and the other salt not appear?

6. Heat a little strong nitric acid in a test-tube, then cautiously drop into it a little turpentine, $C_{10}H_{16}$.

7. Repeat the experiment but use benzine, C_6H_6

8. Place a little carbolic acid in a test-tube, then pour in a few drops of fuming nitric acid. The carbolic acid must be largely diluted, and the tube turned so that the fluid will do no harm if it spurts out.

Explanation.—The staining of organic substances yellow by nitric acid is probably due to the formation of picric acid, a deep yellow dye. When nitric acid acted on carbolic acid the result was picric acid ; the replacement is interesting :

$$C_6H_6O + 3HNO_3 = C_6H_3(NO_2)_3 + 3H_2O + O.$$

9. Assuming that air is by volume 21% oxygen and 79% nitrogen, calculate the weight of a litre of air, and find a multiplier which would enable one to change the specific gravity of a gas from air = 1 to H = 1.

10. Will a metallic nitrate, such as that of copper or zinc, when distilled with sulphuric acid yield nitric acid?

11. Pour some dilute nitric acid on some powdered marble, $CaCO_3$. After the powder disappears, evaporate, test the solid to find if it is a nitrate, then try if it will yield nitric acid when distilled with sulphuric acid.

For nitric acid and nitrates, consult Bloxam, p. 167 ; Muir & Slater, 159; Richter, 203 ; R. & S., 399 ; R., 277 ; Fownes, 152.

CHAPTER XXII.

1.—Avogadro's Law.

Gaseous bodies have their volumes altered by changes in temperature and pressure. Thus the volume occupied by a quantity of gas varies inversely as the pressure to which it is subjected (Boyle's Law); and the volume of a gas varies directly as the absolute temperature (Law of

Charles). Since all gases, whether light or heavy, elementary or compound, vary according to these two laws, it follows that the change must be dependent, not on the chemical, but on the physical properties of gaseous substances. Decrease of volume by compression and increase of volume caused by increase of temperature are both due to the overcoming of molecular forces of attraction and repulsion. It follows, then, that if exactly similar forces cause equal changes in equal volumes of different gases, that equal forces are being overcome ; but equal forces exist only among equal numbers of molecules ; hence the law enunciated by Avogadro, an Italian chemist, which is as follows : *Equal volumes of gases, whether of the same or of different kinds, contain equal numbers of molecules, under like conditions of temperature and pressure.*

Of course this law has not been demonstrated true, but it seems to follow directly not only from the physical reasons already given, but also from the atomic theory. We know from experiment that two volumes of hydrogen unite with one volume of oxygen to form two volumes of steam. If, then, elementary matter is composed of atoms or groups of atoms, there must be two of these individuals or groups of hydrogen in steam for every one that there is of oxygen ; but the volume of the hydrogen is double that of the oxygen ; hence, in equal volumes there must be equal numbers of atoms, or of groups of atoms. (Some reasons for believing that these are groups, that is, molecules, and not individual atoms will be found in Chap. XXXVIII).

CHAPTER XXIII.

1.—Nitrogen and Hydrogen.

There is one well known compound of nitrogen and hydrogen—ammonia, which is of very common occurrence in compounds, and which is of considerable economic importance on account of its use in the arts. This substance has been prepared synthetically in small quantities by passing an electric discharge through a mixture of the two gases of which it is composed. This method of preparation is only of theoretical value, and, as it is not suited for class work, no further reference will be made to it. The ordinary preparation of ammonia and its chief properties will be illustrated by the following experiments.

2.

EXPERIMENTS.

1. Take about 20 grams of dry ammonic chloride and an equal quantity of dry quick-lime; powder them finely in a mortar. Smell the mixture, and then transfer it to a flask with tightly-fitting cork and long tube bent upwards. Heat gently. Hold a large test-tube over the delivery tube, and fill it with gas by downward displacement of air, as in Fig. 32.

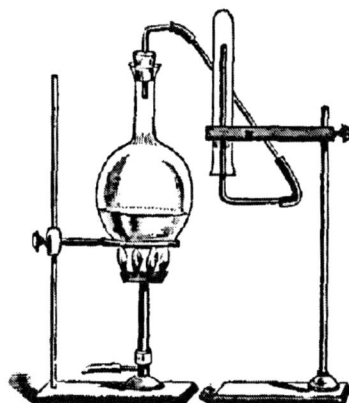

FIG. 32.

$$2NH_4Cl + CaO = CaCl_2 + 2NH_3 + H_2O.$$

2. Pass a lighted taper up into the test-tube full of gas.

3. Pass some of the gas into reddened litmus. Upon the result of this, devise a means of knowing when a bottle is full of this gas.

4. Pour 4 or 5 drops of hydrochloric acid into a large beaker and, by shaking, spread the acid over the bottom and sides of the vessel, then hold it mouth downwards over the delivery tube.

A more convenient method of obtaining ammonia gas is by heating the spirits of hartshorn, the *liquor ammoniæ* of the drug shops. Hartshorn is only a solution of ammonia gas in water.

5. Fit a flask with a rubber stopper and tube as in Fig. 33. Place in the flask a little hartshorn and heat it to boiling. When ammonia gas begins to escape from the tube, invert it, and place the open end in some water coloured pink with litmus.

6. Fill a graduated tube, such as a eudiometer, with dried ammonia gas over mercury, then lift the tube and place it mouth downward in cold water.

7. Fill a large test-tube with ammonia gas over mercury. Take a piece of porous charcoal (that from pine wood, or pine bark is best),

Fig. 33.

hold it in a flame until it begins to burn over most of its surface, then pass it into the tube without raising the latter out of the mercury; let the whole stand for a couple of hours. Is the result due to any action of the mercury?

8. Fit up a piece of apparatus as is shown in Fig. 34.

The tube, A, is a large test-tube drawn out to a nozzle about ⅜ of an inch in diameter, the tube, B, must slide somewhat freely through the per-

Fig. 34.

foration in the stopper and just project beyond the opening in A; C is connected with an oxygen supply, and B is joined to the flask in which ammonia is generated. When the current of ammonia is passing through B try to light it, then turn on the oxygen and after it is escaping from the nozzle try again to ignite the ammonia.

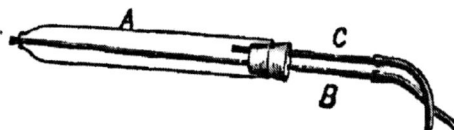

Vary the experiment by passing ammonia through C and oxygen through B, but pull B backwards until its end is just inside the nozzle of A.

Vary the experiment again by pulling B backwards until it projects through the cork only as far as C does; as the mixed gases escape from the nozzle try to ignite them.

Explanation.—When ammonia burns with oxygen it is decomposed, thus :—

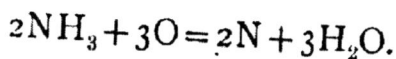

$$2NH_3 + 3O = 2N + 3H_2O.$$

When slowly oxidized, it forms ammonium nitrite and water, thus :—

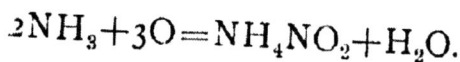

$$2NH_3 + 3O = NH_4NO_2 + H_2O.$$

This is the result of two separate chemical actions though, which are :—

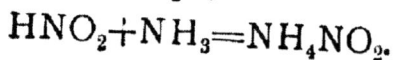

$$NH_3 + 3O = HNO_2 + H_2O, \text{ and}$$
$$HNO_2 + NH_3 = NH_4NO_2.$$

In the former, ammonia unites with oxygen to form nitrous acid and water, then in the latter this nitrous acid combines with part of the free ammonia to form ammonium nitrite.

9. Form about a foot of platinum wire into a spiral by winding it around a lead pencil or bit of glass rod. Heat some hartshorn in a flask until ammonia is coming off, then heat the wire red hot and suspend it in the escaping gas. If kept in the neck of the flask just where the ammonia and air are mixed the spiral should glow for several minutes, while in the air it almost instantly cools.

The explanation is that the red hot platinum promotes the union of the ammonia and the oxygen of the air, the resultant products being those of the combustion of ammonia, and the heat developed in the chemical action is sufficient to keep the platinum at the glowing point.

10. Put about 2 c.c. of dilute hydrochloric acid into a test-tube, pass into this ammonia gas until it is neutral to litmus, then evaporate, but without heating more than is necessary.

11. Vary ex. 10 by dropping hartshorn very *slowly* into hydrochloric acid until it is neutral to litmus, then evaporating. Compare the results in this and in the preceding experiment with that obtained in experiment 4.

3.—Questions and Exercises.

1. How can you tell when a jar is full of this gas, if you collect by displacement of air?

2. Powder some soft coal coarsely in a mortar. Then place in a

hard glass tube and heat. Smell the gas that comes off. Is the liquid that forms acid or alkaline?

3. What became of the ammonia in ex. 7? How could it be shown that mercury did not cause the change?

4. Pass a current of oxygen from a gas holder into an open flask containing hartshorn, warm the latter and apply a light to the mixed gases that are escaping from its mouth.

4.—Ammonium and Ammonium Hydroxide.

The radical NH_4 in ammonium salts is very similar to the metal potassium in its chemical characteristics, and it is generally believed that this unisolated base has the properties of an alkaline metal. The following experiment illustrates one of the reasons for believing in the existence of such a substance. Mercury forms peculiar combinations with many metals; these combinations are not definite in quantity, and seem to be a sort of connecting link between mixtures and chemical compounds. They are exactly analogous to solutions and are called amalgams. Ammonium amalgam can be easily prepared; and as amalgams are formed only with metals, it would seem that ammonium belongs to that class of substances.

EXPERIMENT.

Make a strong solution of ammonium chloride in a beaker and put some sodium amalgam into it. The mass should rapidly swell up to many times its former bulk, have a soapy feeling when rubbed, and give off bubbles of gas that smell strongly of ammonia. After a few hours the original mercury will be found in the beaker and the fluid will have a salty taste.

The reaction may be represented as follows, but the sign '×' must be understood as indicating that the elements whose symbols it joins have formed an amalgam, and this not necessarily in the proportion of one to one :—

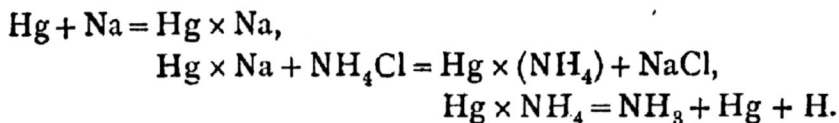

$$Hg + Na = Hg \times Na,$$
$$Hg \times Na + NH_4Cl = Hg \times (NH_4) + NaCl,$$
$$Hg \times NH_4 = NH_3 + Hg + H.$$

Ammonium Hydrate.

When potassium is thrown on water, the water molecules are broken up into hydroxyl molecules and hydrogen, the former uniting with the potassium to form potassic hydrate, and the latter escaping as free gas. It is generally considered that ammonium hydrate is the basic substance that unites with acids to form salts. It has the composition NH_4OH, that is, ammonium in union with hydroxyl. When ammonia gas, NH_3 dissolves in water this hydrate is produced, thus :—

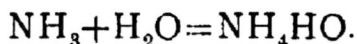

$$NH_3 + H_2O = NH_4HO.$$

It will be necessary to keep very clearly in mind that when compounds of this substance are formed they are compounds of *ammonium*, not of the gas ammonia.

5.—Detection of Ammonia.

It is of importance that ammonia should be capable of easy and accurate detection, as its presence in water, to any appreciable extent, is usually an indication of the unfitness of that water for drinking. The following form the tests generally applied : —

1. Pungent smell, if present in quantity.

2. Dissolve any ammonic salt in water, pour into this solution, in a test-tube, some solution of potassic, sodic or calcic hydrate, then heat, and the odour of ammonia should be perceived.

3. When present in minute quantities, as it frequently is in drinking water, ammonia is best detected by what is known as Nessler's test: "To a solution of potassic iodide add solution of mercuric chloride until the precipitate formed just ceases to be re-dissolved, then add an equal volume of strong solution of caustic potash, and allow the whole to stand until clear. A few drops of this solution will give a yellowish-red precipitate, with even the slightest trace of ammonia."

6.—Notes on Ammonia.

Ammonia: symbol, NH_3; mol. vol., 2; vapour density, 8.5.

Ammonium is a *strongly alkaline, monad base.*

Ammonia is soluble to upwards of 700 times its bulk in water at 15°C; it becomes a liquid at—40°C, and may even be frozen at—75°C.

It occurs in the urine and in some other products of animals; also in air as the result of the decay or decomposition of nitrogenous animal matter, hence it exists in rain water. Its compounds, ammonium chloride and ammonium carbonate, are found sparingly in nature.

It is prepared for commercial purposes from the waste products of gas works. The illuminating gas, after coming from the retort, is washed in cold water to free it from soluble impurities; the ammonia is thus dissolved and afterwards separated as the chloride.

Dilute liquor ammoniæ is used in medical practice and in manufactures to neutralize acids. Its compounds are used in medicine as stimulants in cases of fainting or of syncope from overdoses of chloroform, ether or laughing gas. It is also used in dyeing. The latent heat resulting from its volatility, renders it valuable for cooling purposes in some manufactures.

7.—Questions and Exercises.

1. Complete the following equations :—

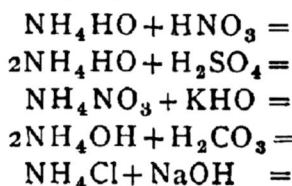

$$NH_4HO + HNO_3 =$$
$$2NH_4HO + H_2SO_4 =$$
$$NH_4NO_3 + KHO =$$
$$2NH_4OH + H_2CO_3 =$$
$$NH_4Cl + NaOH =$$

2. Potassic chloride and potassic nitrate are written KCl and KNO_3 respectively, while ammonia has the formula NH_3, but the chloride and nitrate are written NH_4Cl and NH_4NO_3. How is the extra atom of hydrogen accounted for ?

3. Ammonium nitrate has its formula written NH_4NO_3, what objection is there to writing it $N_2H_4O_3$?

4. What weight of ammonia gas at 60°. F. can be obtained from 214 grams of ammonic chloride ?

5. What weight of quick-lime is required to decompose 107 grams of ammonic chloride, and what will be the weight of the calcic chloride and water produced ? What weight of ammonia gas will be evolved ?

6. Ammonium chloride is heated with caustic soda, the resultant gas led into water, this solution neutralized with nitric acid, then evaporated to dryness, and heated in a test-tube until decomposed. Write the equations for the various steps of this process.

8.—Additional Exercises.

The combining power of substances in the nascent state is well shown by the formation of ammonia, as illustrated by the following experiments :—

1. Make a mixture of hydrogen and nitrogen. Try by testing with litmus and by smelling the gas if any trace of ammonia can be detected.

2. Mix in a mortar 30 centigrams of fine iron filings with sixty centigrams of solid caustic potash. Then transfer the mixture to a test-tube fitted with cork and delivery tube, and heat until gas escapes. Collect some of this gas and test for hydrogen.

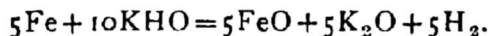

$$5Fe + 10KHO = 5FeO + 5K_2O + 5H_2.$$

Iron and caustic potash yield ferrous oxide, potassic oxide and hydrogen.

3. Repeat the experiment, substituting 20 centigrams of nitre for the 60 of potash. In this case test for nitrogen.

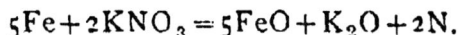

$$5Fe + 2KNO_3 = 5FeO + K_2O + 2N.$$

Iron and potassic nitrate give ferrous oxide, potassic oxide and nitrogen.

4. Now mix 30 centigrams of iron filings, 30 of caustic potash and 6 of nitre, place in a test-tube and heat as before. Smell the gas that is evolved.

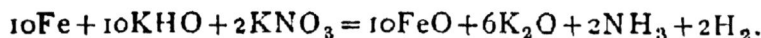

$$10Fe + 10KHO + 2KNO_3 = 10FeO + 6K_2O + 2NH_3 + 2H_2.$$

Iron, potassic hydrate and potassic nitrate yield ferrous oxide, potassic oxide, ammonia and water—the ammonia instead of free hydrogen and free nitrogen ; though free hydrogen and nitrogen, when formed separately and then mixed, will not form ammonia.

5. Pass ammonia for some time into a long test-tube of ice cold water. Note any changes in temperature and volume of the water.

8

9.—Determination of the Composition of Ammonia.

1. Take a eudiometer, fill it with mercury and invert over a small trough or saucer, also containing mercury. Heat some ammonium hydrate and pass 20 c. c. of the gas into the eudiometer. Then pass a series of electric sparks from an induction coil through the gas, taking care to insert a Leyden jar in the circuit, so as to increase the heating effect. When the gas no longer expands, pass 30 cc. of pure oxygen into the eudiometer and explode. Depress the eudiometer so as to bring the mercury to the same level inside and outside ; then note the volume of the gas remaining in it.

———

10.—Questions and Exercises.

1. What must be the composition of the gases remaining after the explosion? What volume of each? What then are the constituents of ammonia by volume?

2. How many atoms of each element must there be in the molecule of ammonia? What therefore must be its formula?

3. Assuming the truth of Avogadro's Law, what space does the molecule of ammonia occupy as compared with that of an atom of hydrogen?

4. In performing Ex. 5, sec. 2, the bottom of the flask broke into small pieces, but these all flew *inwards*. How may such a result be accounted for?

5. In preparing ammonia from sal ammoniac and lime, try if it will answer to make the substances into a paste with water.

6. Into some dilute sulphuric acid in a test-tube put some pieces of zinc, after hydrogen begins to come off freely, add drop by drop some nitric acid until the gas ceases to pass out of the liquid. Then add potassic hydrate and heat. Ammonia should escape. How may its formation be accounted for?

7. Place a small piece of ammonium chloride upon a strip of platinum foil and heat for some time. Devise an experiment to determine whether the change is a physical one or a chemical one.

8. How many volumes of ammonia will be produced by uniting one volume of nitrogen and three volumes of hydrogen? Upon what experimental evidence is the answer based?

9. It is said that any ammoniacal salt heated with any alkaline hydrate or oxide will yield ammonia. Try with as many of the following as you can get, and write the equation for the reaction, in each case in which the gas is obtained :—

(a) Ammonium nitrate, NH_4NO_3, with potassic hydrate KHO.
(b) Ammonium carbonate $(NH_4)_2CO_3$, with barium oxide BaO.
(c) Ammonium sulphate $(NH_4)_2SO_4$, with calcium hydrate $Ca(OH)_2$.
(d) Ammonium chloride NH_4Cl, with sodium hydrate NaOH.

10. Pour some hartshorn into a beaker and place a thermometer in it to get its temperature. Tie a piece of cloth or filtering paper loosely about the lower end of the thermometer, then let a few drops of this same hartshorn run down the stem and drip through the cloth or paper. Compare the fall in temperature with that when alchohol, water, ether, or chloroform is used.

CHAPTER XXIV.

PERCENTAGE COMPOSITION AND FORMULÆ.

1.—To Calculate the Formula of a Compound when its Percentage Composition is Known.

As soon as we have determined what elements are present in an unknown compound, and what their relative weights are, we can use this knowledge to construct a formula which will show the molecular composition of the substance. For instance, a gaseous compound may yield oxygen and nitrogen on analysis, but this does not settle what oxide of nitrogen it is.

Some examples worked out will make clear the methods of solution and the principles on which they are based.

Examples.

1. A certain compound when analyzed yielded sodium 27%, nitrogen 16·5%, oxygen 56·5%. What is its formula? The percentages give the relative weights of the constituents in a unit weight of the compound; therefore the relative weights of the different kinds of atoms in a molecule of the compound. In a molecule of this compound, if the weight of the sodium atoms be represented by 27, that of the nitrogen will be 16½, and that of the oxygen 56½. We must next find the *relative numbers* of these atoms in the molecule. To do this the percentage weight must be divided by the atomic weight of the element.

$$Sodium, \quad 27 \quad \div 23 = 1.17 \pm.$$
$$Nitrogen, \quad 16 \quad \div 14 = 1.17 \pm.$$
$$Oxygen, \quad 56.5 \div 16 = 3.5 \ \pm.$$

We now know that for every 1·17 atoms of sodium there are 1·17 atoms of nitrogen and 3·5 atoms of oxygen. These figures are not absolutely correct, but in practical work, errors of experiment render mathematical accuracy an impossibility. The next step will be to determine what *integral numbers* will express these ratios. To do this, we divide the smallest of the quotients obtained in the last operation into each of the others.

Thus, for sodium, $\frac{1\cdot17}{1\cdot17} = 1.$

" nitrogen, $\frac{1\cdot17}{1\cdot17} = 1.$

" oxygen, $\frac{3\cdot5}{1\cdot17} = 3.$

This tells us that the numbers of atoms of sodium, nitrogen and oxygen are as 1, 1 and 3. Hence the formula for the compound is $NaNO_3$, or some multiple of this, $n(NaNO_3)$

2. A compound gave on analysis 78·3% silver, 4·3% carbon, 17·4% oxygen. Find a formula for it.

Solution.

$78.3 \div 108 = .725 \; ; \; 4.3 \div 12 = .358 \; ; \; 17.4 \div 16 = 1.09.$

$$.725 \div .358 = 2 \pm$$
$$.358 \div .358 = 1$$
$$1.09 \div .358 = 3 \pm.$$

There are, therefore, two atoms of silver to one of carbon to three of oxygen. Hence a formula for the substance is Ag_2CO_3. This is not necessarily the exact formula, because $Ag_4C_2O_6$ or $Ag_{2n}C_nO_{3n}$ would answer just as well, so far as the data of the question applies. There is an element left out in stating the problem which is necessary for an exact solution. This is the vapour density, which will be dealt with in another chapter. For present practice, the lowest number of atoms permissible may be taken as the proper formula, which is then said to be **empirical.**

Definition.

An **empirical formula** expresses the proportions by weight in which the constituents of a substance unite to form it.

The proper empirical formula for each compound substance is fixed by accurate chemical analysis.

To solve all similar problems observe the following rule :

1. Divide the percentage amount of each constituent element by its own atomic weight.

2. Divide each of the quotients thus obtained by the lowest of them and the numbers obtained will express the proportional number of atoms of each element in the compound.

Exercise.

The following are percentage compositions of various substances ; determine a formula for each.

1. Carbon, 42·86 ; oxygen, 57··14.
2. Hydrogen, 2·73 ; chlorine, 97·27.
3. Hydrogen, ·83 ; sodium, 19·17 ; sulphur, 26·66 ; oxygen, 53·33
4. Sodium, 39·31 ; chlorine, 60·69.
5. Nitrogen, 82·35 ; hydrogen, 17·65.
6. Phosphorus, 91·17 ; hydrogen, 8·83.
7. Carbon, 26·67 ; hydrogen, 2·22 ; oxygen, 71·11.
8. Carbon, 75 ; hydrogen, 25.
9. Carbon, 12 ; calcium, 40 ; oxygen, 48.

10. ·9 gram of a substance containing carbon, hydrogen and oxygen is found on analysis to yield ·24 gram of carbon and ·02 of hydrogen. Calculate its simplest formula.

11. ·9 gram of a substance containing carbon, oxygen and hydrogen is found on analysis to yield ·06 of hydrogen and ·48 of oxygen. Calculate its simplest formula.

12. A portion of a substance is found on analysis to yield ·36 gram of carbon, ·055 gram of hydrogen, and ·44 of oxygen. Calculate its formula.

2.—To Calculate Percentage Composition from the Formula.

Sometimes we are given the formula of a substance and are asked to calculate the percentage composition. This is easily done. Proceed as follows :—

Find the molecular weight of the compound by taking the sum of the atomic weights of its constituents, then divide this separately into the weights of the atoms of the different elements in the molecule.

Example.

Calculate the percentage composition of sulphate of copper, $CuSO_4$.

$$
\begin{array}{ll}
\text{Copper} \dotfill & 63 \cdot 5 \\
\text{Sulphur} \dotfill & 32 \\
\text{Oxygen } (16 \times 4) \dotfill & 64 \\
\hline
& 159 \cdot 5
\end{array}
$$

If, by weight, in $159\frac{1}{2}$ parts of sulphate of copper there are $63\frac{1}{2}$ parts of copper, how many parts by weight of the metal will there be in 100 of sulphate.

$159\frac{1}{2}$ of sulphate yield $\quad 63\frac{1}{2}$ of copper.

$\therefore$ I will yield . . . . $\dfrac{63\frac{1}{2}}{159\frac{1}{2}}$

and $\therefore$ 100 will yield . . $\dfrac{63 \cdot 5}{159 \cdot 5} \times \dfrac{100}{1} = 39.81$ per cent.

The percentage of sulphur and oxygen in this compound may be found in the same way.

Exercise.

What is the percentage composition of each of the following substances :—

1. Arsenious oxide, As_2O_3.
2. Chloride of gold, $AuCl_3$.
3. Arseniuretted hydrogen, AsH_3.
4. Potassium ferrocyanide, $K_4FeC_6N_6$.
5. Magnesium sulphate, $MgSO_4$.
6. Copper nitrate, $Cu(NO_3)_2$.

3.—Graphic and Rational Formulæ.

Rational Formulæ.—A rational formula besides expressing the proportions by weight in which the elements are united, expresses also the way in which the elements are supposed to be grouped within the molecule of a compound. For example,

$$\left.\begin{array}{l} HO \\ HO \end{array}\right\} SO_2$$ is the rational formula for sulphuric acid,—that

is, two hydroxyl molecules joined with sulphur dioxide.

Graphic Formulæ.—Graphic formulæ express more fully than rational formulæ the manner in which we suppose atoms to be associated in forming compounds. For example, the graphic formula for water is H—O—H.

For nitric acid the empirical formula is HNO_3; the rational formula is $NO_2(OH)$, and the graphic formula,

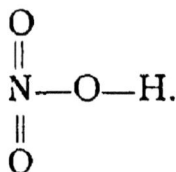

$$\begin{array}{c} O \\ \| \\ N{-}O{-}H. \\ \| \\ O \end{array}$$

In graphic formulæ, the lines indicate the manner in which the atomicities of each element are disposed of;

nitrogen being joined to the other elements by five links, oxygen by two, and hydrogen by one.

In the formula for water, oxygen is shown to be a diad, because it has two combining powers joining it to the two atoms of hydrogen. In a similar way, nitrogen is a pentad, each atom of oxygen a diad and hydrogen a monad.

The graphic formula for sulphuric acid may be written

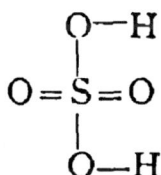

$$\begin{array}{c} \text{O---H} \\ | \\ \text{O} = \text{S} = \text{O} \\ | \\ \text{O---H} \end{array}$$

The graphic formulæ for ammonic chloride, ammonic nitrate, copper sulphate, copper nitrate, are respectively:

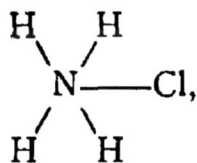

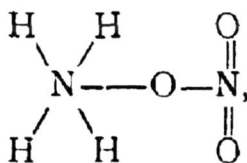

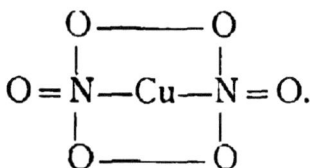

Exercises.

Construct graphic formulæ for hydrogen peroxide, ozone, potassic nitrate, sodium hydrate, calcic hydrate, $Ca(OH)_2$, acid sulphate of potassium, zinc sulphate, potassic chlorate.

CHAPTER XXV.

1.—Carbon.

This element enters into the composition of every organic substance, and is a constituent of a very large number of mineral substances. It exists in three forms that, physically, are entirely different from one another, but chemically are identical.

The word **allotropism** is used to express the fact that some elements exist in very unlike states physically, or with very different properties, but all the while preserve their fundamental chemical identity.

The allotropic forms of carbon are (1) **charcoal**, an impure form derived by roasting organic matters out of contact with air; (2) **graphite, plumbago** or **black lead,** a mineral found chiefly in metamorphic rocks; and (3) **diamond.** The last is the purest form.

2.—Experiments with Charcoal.

1. Partly fill a narrow test-tube with white paper, dry sawdust, or pieces of dry wood; stop the mouth loosely with a piece of chalk, or pour sand to a depth of half an inch over the substance in the tube. Hold the tube in a nearly horizontal position with its lower end in a lamp-flame. As the heating goes on, notice whether any odour is evolved. Place separate pieces of blue and red litmus paper within the mouth of the tube. When nearly all action has ceased, turn out and examine what remains in the test-tube.

2. Place a little of the residue on platinum foil, or on a sheet of mica, and heat over a lamp flame for some time. Observe what is left.

3. Clean as well as you can the test-tube used in the preceding experiment, and then repeat it, using a piece of woollen cloth, silk cloth, or dry lean meat.

4. Heat on a sheet of mica the residue obtained in experiment 3.

5. Heat some sugar upon a sheet of mica.

6. Place a wet filter paper inside a funnel, and then cover the inside of the filter paper with a thick coating of animal charcoal or bone black. Now filter through the paper a wine-glassful of ale or porter, or a solution of dark brown sugar.

Definition.

Roasting a substance out of contact with air is known as **destructive distillation** of it.

3.—Questions and Exercises.

1. How is wood charcoal prepared? Animal charcoal? Is wood an element? Give reasons for your answer.

2. Mention one difference between the liquid produced in the destructive distillation of wood and that obtained in the destructive distillation of lean meat.

3. Charcoal is said to be an impure form of carbon. What impurities have you found? Is the statement regarding impurity true of animal, as well as of wood charcoal?

4. Put into an alcohol lamp a mixture of fluids, two-thirds alcohol and one-third turpentine. Hold a cold plate in its flame until a thick coating of soot is formed on it, scrape this coating off and heat it on mica. This black powder is **lamp-black**. Is it carbon?

5. Set fire to one corner of a sheet of paper and let it slowly burn away, then try if the charred sheet will again burn. What is finally left?

6. Let a piece of meat stand until it begins to smell putrid, then cover it with powdered charcoal. How is the foul smell affected? How long does this continue?

7. Ascertain what effect animal charcoal has upon solutions of (a) litmus, (b) indigo, (c) potassium permanganate, (d) writing ink, when these fluids are filtered through it.

8. Fill a test-tube with air over mercury, pass into the tube a piece of freshly-burned charcoal and let the whole stand for an hour.

9. Water filters are frequently made of layers of sand and charcoal laid alternately. From your experiments, have you reason to believe that this would prove a serviceable arrangement? Would it be likely to be *permanently* effective?

4.—Additional Exercises.

1. Place a piece of charcoal in a test-tube and then pour upon it a little strong sulphuric acid. Observe whether the charcoal changes in any way. Try whether an alkali will produce any change in the charcoal.

2. Wet the inside of a large test-tube with liquor ammoniæ. Now drop into the tube some wood charcoal previously heated in a covered crucible. Cork the tube, and after a few minutes remove the cork and ascertain by smelling whether there is any ammonia left in the test-tube.

3. Secure a piece of electric-light carbon; try if it will burn (1) in an ordinary flame, (2) in a blowpipe flame.

4. Heat, in a test-tube, a piece of soft coal covered with a layer of sand. Does it undergo destructive distillation? Try with hard coal.

5. Cut two little blocks of wood about as large as peas. Heat one of these over a flame on a piece of mica; notice what is left after all action ceases.

Heat the other similarly on a piece of mica, but take the precaution to cover it to a depth of half an inch with some incombustible substance like sand, clay, chalk-dust or lime.

6. Repeat the last experiment, but substitute lean meat for wood.

7. From a sample of coarse brown sugar prepare some that will be pure and white.

8. Devise an experiment to ascertain how long charcoal will retain its decolorizing and deodorizing power when in use as a deodorant.

9. If, after animal black has lost its power as a decolorizer, it were again roasted, would it regain that power? Test your conjecture by an experiment.

Definition.—A substance which has the power of destroying offensive smells is called a **deodorant.**

CHAPTER XXVI.

1.—Carbon and Oxygen.

There are two well-known oxides of carbon, viz., carbon monoxide (carbonic oxide), and carbon dioxide (carbonic anhydride, carbonic acid gas, or choke damp). The latter is of general distribution in the atmosphere; and, dissolved in water, has played a very important part in the formation of the rocky crust of the earth. It is also necessary for the support of vegetable life.

2.—Carbon Dioxide.

The test for the presence of this gas is *lime water.* This is prepared by pouring clean water on lime, letting it stand for several hours, with frequent stirring, then allowing it to settle and decanting the clear liquid. This should have a distinct alkaline taste, and should be free from turbidity. When carbon dioxide is passed through lime water a white precipitate is thrown down.

EXPERIMENTS.

1. Twist one end of a piece of fine wire round a bit of charcoal, hold the latter in a lamp flame until it is glowing brightly, then lower it into a bottle and insert the cork beside the wire ; when the charcoal ceases to burn withdraw it and shake up some lime water with the gas in the bottle. Contrive a means of driving the gas in the bottle through lime water in a test-tube.

2. Take the apparatus used in preparing hydrogen and in it place some powdered limestone or white marble. Then cover the marble with water, and pour down the thistle-tube some hydrochloric acid. Collect, over the pneumatic trough, two or three bell jars and two or three large test-tubes full of the gas. The equation for the re-action is

$$CaCO_3 + 2HCl = CaCl_2 + H_2O + CO_2.$$

3. Test the gas by lowering into it a lighted candle. Substitute a piece of burning phosphorus for the candle.

4. Invert one of the test-tubes full of the gas over water and let it stand for some hours.

5. Test, with litmus, the water that rises in the tube, in the previous experiment. This may be done by slipping the hand under the mouth of the tube, then raising the whole and inverting it. If the litmus is not immediately changed, let it stand for a time.

6. Invert a tube full of carbon dioxide over mercury, then with a curved pipette pass a solution of potassic hydrate up into the tube. Vary the experiment by trying to collect the gas over a solution of caustic potash.

3.—Questions and Exercises.

1. Devise experiments to show that carbon dioxide is formed in (a) a burning lamp, (b) burning coal gas.

2. Show, by means of the lime water test, that this gas is given off during respiration.

3. It is said that carbon dioxide is one of the common impurities of ill-ventilated school rooms. Devise a means of testing the accuracy of this statement.

4. What is the gas that comes off from ginger ale, soda water or ale when the bottle is unstopped? To find out, prepare a cork with a delivery tube that will fit the neck of the bottle, then unstop the bottle and quickly insert the prepared cork ; allow the escaping gas to pass through lime water. Why does the gas escape with a rush when the cork is drawn ?

5. Twenty-five grams of sodium carbonate is heated with just enough dilute hydrochloric acid to complete the chemical action ; the gas that comes off is passed into solution of ammonia which is afterwards evaporated to dryness.

(a) Write the equation for the reaction.

(b) If the hydrochloric acid were 25% pure, what weight of it would be required? (Ordinary hydrochloric acid may be assumed to be a 20% solution by weight of the gaseous acid in water.)

(c) What weight of each of the salts would be formed ?

6. Mention substances that when burned do not yield carbonic acid gas as one of the products of combustion.

7. Lime water is a solution of calcic hydrate, $Ca(HO)_2$. This in contact with carbon dioxide forms calcic carbonate ; thus :

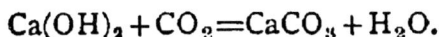

$$Ca(OH)_2 + CO_2 = CaCO_3 + H_2O.$$

Calcic carbonate may take the form of limestone, marble or chalk. It is called by the last name when in fine white powder.

Is chalk dust soluble in water ? Is sodium carbonate soluble in water? From your observations, tell why a solution of calcic hydrate rather than a solution of sodic hydrate is used as the test for carbon dioxide.

4.—Additional Exercises.

1. Hang, by a piece of bent wire, a lighted taper with a small flame in a gas cylinder, then pour carbon dioxide into this cylinder, out of another vessel. Try to pour carbon dioxide upwards into a jar, then test with lime water to see if the gas really passed into the upper vessel.

2. Try if this gas can be prepared from any of the following salts when treated with any one of the acids given : Ammonium carbonate $(NH_4)_2CO_3$, sodium bicarbonate, $NaHCO_3$, potassium carbonate, K_2CO_3, ammonium bicarbonate $(NH_4)HCO_3$, lead carbonate, $PbCO_3$ (white lead, $PbCO_3 PbOH$ will do), barium carbonate, $BaCO_3$; for acid, either dilute nitric, dilute hydrochloric or dilute sulphuric may be taken. In each case write the equation.

3. Take a large bottle, to hold a gallon if possible, fill it with water ; and, in the worst ventilated room in the school, empty this water into another vessel. Have ready a large test-tube full of lime water, pour this into the bottle, cork the latter and shake the lime water thoroughly with the air, then pour it back into the test-tube. Repeat the experiment, but collect the air outside the building and use an equal quantity of fresh lime water. Compare the quantity of precipitate in the two tubes.

4. Counterpoise a large beaker on a scale, then pass a stream of carbon dioxide into this beaker. How is the scale affected ? How can you tell when the beaker is full of the gas ?

5. Try whether you can syphon carbon dioxide from one jar to another ?

5.—Solution of Calcic Carbonate in Solution of Carbon Dioxide.

A fact of immense importance in the history of the world is that a solution of carbon dioxide in water is capable of dissolving limestone which is insoluble in pure water. The following experiments illustrate this.

1. Pass a current of carbon dioxide through lime water until the precipitate formed at first nearly all dissolves. Filter and divide the filtrate into several parts. Boil one of them, it should turn milky in appearance. Drop into another a little ammonia; into another, some potassic hydrate solution; into another, some more lime water. A white precipitate should be formed in each case.

Explanation.

When the carbon dioxide is first passed into the lime water a precipitate of calcic carbonate, $CaCO_3$, is thrown down; when the water becomes saturated with the dioxide this precipitate is dissolved; perhaps because of the formation of an acid carbonate, $CaH_2(CO_3)_2$; but any treatment that takes the carbon dioxide out of the solution causes the precipitate to be again formed, because water alone will not dissolve the neutral carbonate. Boiling expels the carbonic acid gas, and the alkaline hydrates unite with it to form other carbonates.

The quantity of carbon dioxide that water will dissolve varies as the pressure to which the water is subjected, hence, springs that come from far below the surface sometimes contain much of this gas dissolved, and if the solution has trickled over limestone the latter will be also dissolved and carried to the surface, where it will be

9

deposited, because, the pressure being removed from the water, the dioxide escapes.

From what has been shown in the preceding experiments can you explain the cause of the deposition of "lime" (furring) of steam boilers, tea kettles and other vessels in which much water has been boiled?

———

6.—Reducing Power of Carbon.

Carbon is very largely used in metallurgy as a reducing agent, the monoxide, and dioxide being formed in the process. The following experiments illustrate the principle on which it acts.

1. Mix in a hard glass tube, closed at one end, some copper oxide and powdered charcoal; on top of this place a thick layer of charcoal, then heat strongly. Test the gas coming off for carbon dioxide. Examine what remains in the tube.

2. Repeat the preceding experiment but use arsenic trioxide for copper oxide. What appears on the cold part of the tube?

3. Try if red lead and iron rust are changed, when subjected to treatment similar to that applied to the copper oxide.

———

7.—Carbonic Acid.

It has been found in previous experiments that when carbon dioxide, prepared either from burning carbon, or from the decomposition of a carbonate, is dissolved in water, it forms a distinctly acid solution. The solution is dilute **carbonic acid,** formed thus :—$H_2O + CO_2 = H_2CO_3$. The acid cannot be obtained in a concentrated form, because it readily breaks up again into water and carbon dioxide. Though the acid is thus unstable, its salts are of very general occurrence, and form a considerable part of the earth's mass. It forms carbonates with all the common metals and alkalies, the most common of these being calcium carbonate in its various forms of chalk, limestone and marble.

All carbonates are very readily decomposed by the action of any strong acid upon them, with the evolution of carbon dioxide gas. Thus :

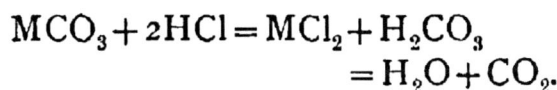

$$MCO_3 + 2HCl = MCl_2 + H_2CO_3$$
$$= H_2O + CO_2.$$

The carbonic acid at once breaks up into water and carbon dioxide. The decomposition of the acid may be represented graphically as follows :

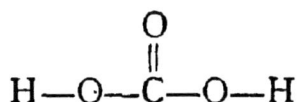

$$\overset{\displaystyle O}{\underset{\displaystyle H-O-C-O-H}{\|}}$$

When the two hydrogen atoms are freed, the two oxygen atoms to which they are attached are thrown into an unstable condition and the result is a rearrangement ; thus :

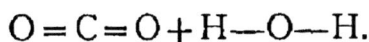

$$O = C = O + H - O - H.$$

The alkaline carbonates alone are soluble in water. Most carbonates when strongly heated break up into carbon dioxide and the oxide of the metal. The well-known burning of limestone to form lime serves as an example.

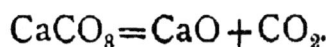

$$CaCO_3 = CaO + CO_2.$$

Experiments.

1. Take a hydrogen generating apparatus and place in it some powdered chalk, or oyster shells. Cover with water. Insert the cork tightly and then pour down the thistle-tube some hydrochloric acid. Collect the gas that escapes and test it for carbon dioxide.

2. The following is a simple method, when you want to prepare quicklime on a small scale; but you need a Bunsen burner with which to do it. Take a piece of calc-spar and round it, wind some platinum wire. Hold the calc-spar in the hottest part of the Bunsen flame for a short time.

3. Moisten a piece of red litmus paper and press it against a piece of limestone or marble. Now press a similar piece of litmus against a piece of recently burnt quicklime.

4. To a lump of quicklime add, little by little, water until it becomes pasty. What became of the first water that was added? What did the change of temperature indicate?

8.—Additional Exercises.

Carbon Dioxide Contains Carbon and Oxygen.

Experiments.

1. Lead a current of carbon dioxide through a hard glass tube which contains some thin slices of sodium. After the gas has been passing long enough to exclude all air from the tube, heat the sodium until it ignites. After a few minutes remove the tube and scrape out the black flakes. Prove that these are carbon by burning them in a current of air and leading the product of combustion through lime water. For this, use the apparatus of Fig. 26, but

insert a bottle of lime water between the aspirator and combustion tube. The white solid left in the tube is sodium oxide, and when dissolved in water it forms sodium hydrate. Test it for sodium.

2. A piece of burning magnesium, if put into carbon dioxide will continue to burn. Try this, and after the combustion has ceased, a little weak nitric acid will dissolve the magnesic oxide and leave the carbon particles.

3. Take thin pieces of marble, chalk or oyster shell, and weigh them. Place them upon an old tin plate, or in a crucible, and heat in a fire to redness, for an hour or two. Remove them and try whether they will now yield carbon dioxide on the addition of hydrochloric acid. The residue after the roasting is called **quicklime**, or simply lime. Note differences in colour and weight between lime and limestone.

***

9.—Notes on Carbon Dioxide.

Carbon dioxide: symbol, CO_2; mol. weight, 44; vapour density, 22; sp. gr., 1·52 (air = 1); soluble to the extent of about 3 vols. of gas in 2 of water; exists in air to the extent of about 4 vols. in 10,000. This supply is maintained by the breath of animals, the combustion of carbonaceous matters, the decomposition of carbonates, and by fermentation.

This gas is the choke damp of miners; so named because of the formation of large quantities of it by the explosion of another gas (fire damp) in the mines, and its deadly effect when breathed continuously. As it contains no free oxygen it is incapable of supporting life, so asphyxiation results if it is inhaled for any length of time. The carbon dioxide in the atmosphere is largely absorbed and decomposed by plants and part of it used by them as a food.

10.—Carbon Monoxide.

EXPERIMENTS.

1. Into a Florence flask put 8 or 10 grams of oxalic acid, and about 50 c. c. of sulphuric acid. Fit with a tight cork and tube and attach, as in Fig. 35, to a wash bottle containing a strong solution of caustic potash. From the wash bottle, a delivery tube should pass to the pneumatic trough. Apply heat cautiously to the flask, regulating it so that the gas may come off in a slow, steady stream. After the

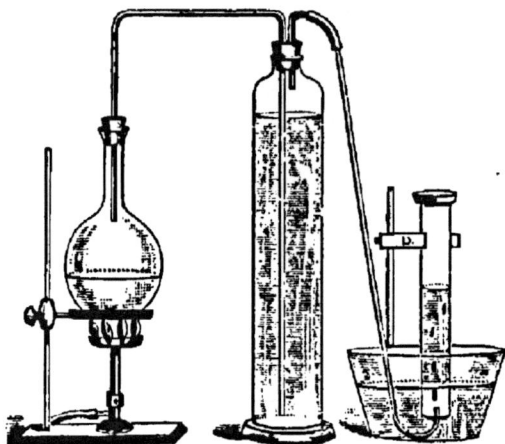

FIG. 35.

air has been expelled from the apparatus, collect three bottles of the gas, and allow these bottles to stand over water for some time before using them. Meanwhile, substitute for the delivery tube one whose end has been drawn to a fine point. Apply a lighted match to the jet.*

2. Raise one of the bottles of gas from the water, and apply a lighted taper to its mouth.

3. Try to pour the gas from one bottle to another, then test the result with a lighted taper.

---

* Unless the experimenter is careful he will get enough carbon dioxide mixed with the monoxide to spoil his result. To guard against this he should use a large volume of the potash solution in a tall vessel, then if necessary he should cause the gas to bubble *slowly* through this a second time, or better still, let it stand for several hours over caustic potash solution.

Carbon monoxide is an exceedingly poisonous gas, therefore should not be inhaled.

4. Purify thoroughly the gas in a third bottle, by shaking it up well with caustic potash or caustic soda solution, then test the gas with clear lime water.

11.—Questions and Exercises.

1. If carbon monoxide burns in air, try to find out whether vapour of water is formed during the process of combustion? Whether carbon dioxide is formed?

2. On what data can you conclude that carbon dioxide contains more oxygen than carbon monoxide?

3. Hydrogen and carbon monoxide are both combustible. Can you conclude from this resemblance that carbon monoxide and oxygen will form an explosive mixture? Test the accuracy of your conclusion.

4. Oxalic acid has the formula of $C_2H_2O_4$, and sulphuric acid takes from this the elements that, when united, form water. Write the equation for the reaction, and explain the necessity for the wash bottle filled with potassic hydrate solution in experiment 1, sec. 10.

5. Try if a burning splinter, or burning phosphorus will continue to burn if thrust into a jar of carbon monoxide.

6. Thirty grams of oxalic acid is treated with excess of sulphuric acid, the resultant gas led through a solution of sodium hydrate in which all the carbon dioxide is dissolved, the remaining gas is burned, and the product of combustion passed into lime water where it unites with the dissolved hydrate. Write equations for the several reactions, and determine what weight of each compound is formed.

7. How do you account for the blue blaze that spreads over coal, when newly thrown on a hot fire?

8. Trace the chemical changes that occur when air enters a furnace by the lower damper, passes through a fire pot filled with white hot coals, into the air space above the coals, thence out through the smoke pipe at the top of the furnace.

9. In what particulars (3 at least) does hydrogen resemble carbon monoxide? How would you distinguish them, if similar jars were filled, one with each gas, and given to you?

12.—Additional Exercises.

1. If we can form carbon dioxide from carbon monoxide by supplying it with oxygen, it ought to be possible to prepare carbon monoxide from carbon dioxide by supplying it with carbon. Test the accuracy of this induction by using apparatus similar to that in Fig. 12, and passing dry carbon dioxide over red-hot charcoal.

2. Pass carbonic oxide and oxyg' 'ito a eudiometer over mercury. Do they unite when an elec . spark is passed through the mixture? How can you tell whether or not a union has taken place?

3. Try if carbonic oxide will burn in nitrous oxide gas.

4. By using the apparatus of Fig. 45 (appendix), or some similar device, drive a current of carbon monoxide through a delivery tube, ignite the escaping gas and allow it to burn under a stoppered bell jar or inverted bottle, whose mouth dips under water. After the combustion ceases, let the jar or bottle stand over a solution of caustic potash for some hours. What gas remains?

CHAPTER XXVII.

1.—Relation Between Volumes of Constituents and the Volume of the Compound Formed, when all are Gases.

We have already seen that 2 volumes of hydrogen unite with 1 of oxygen to form two volumes of steam. The compound formed occupies only $\frac{2}{3}$ of the volume which we would expect it to occupy. The process of union has brought about a *shrinkage* in volume which we must try to understand.

On the other hand, when nitrous oxide is decomposed, we find that 2 volumes of the gas produce 2 volumes of nitrogen and 1 volume of oxygen. In other words, the process of decomposition has given rise to an *increase* of volume. Both these results appear to contradict the well known fact that 2 and 1 make 3, but in reality they are easily understood if we use Avogadro's law as the basis of explanation. According to this law, one molecule of any substance in the gaseous state occupies the same space as one molecule of any other substance under like conditions. Now, the molecules of the mixed gases in the first example, in the process of union, re-arrange their atoms and combine them so that the number of new molecules of steam formed are reduced in the proportion of 3 to 2, and consequently the total number of molecules in the steam is only $\frac{2}{3}$ of what they were in the mixture, hence, as all molecules occupy the same space, the total volume is diminished to $\frac{2}{3}$ of what it was at first.

The very opposite takes place in the decomposition of nitrous oxide. Here the new molecules are increased in number, in the proportion of 3 to 2, and hence the total volume is increased to one half more than in the nitrous oxide.

When we come to study hydrochloric acid we shall find that 1 volume of hydrogen unites with 1 volume of chlorine to form 2 volumes of the gas. Similarly, 2 volumes of nitric oxide may be decomposed into 1 volume of nitrogen and 1 of oxygen. In both these cases, there is neither an increase nor a diminution in volume, because in the re-arrangement of the atoms to form new molecules, the number of molecules in the products are exactly the same as at first.

Stating these results generally : there will be in the final product of any chemical reaction an increase, a diminution, or equality in volume to that which entered into the reaction, according as the atoms re-arrange themselves so as to produce more molecules, fewer molecules, or an equal number of molecules to those which first entered into the reaction. If the number of molecules remain the same at the end of a reaction as at the beginning, the volume will be the same : if the number of molecules has increased, the volume must have increased : and if the number has diminished, the volume must have diminished. In all cases the volume is entirely independent of the number of atoms in each molecule, but depends, as already stated, upon the number of molecules.

1. Apply this principle and explain what change of volume will take place when ammonia and nitrogen trioxide are decomposed.

2. What change in volume, if any, will take place when (a) sulphur is burned in oxygen, (b) carbon dioxide is passed over red-hot charcoal, (c) marsh gas is burned in air? In the first case, devise an experiment to ascertain whether your conclusion is correct or not.

2.—Vapor Density.

The molecule of a gaseous body occupies the space of two atoms of hydrogen (this will be clear if it is remembered that steam when decomposed yields its own volume of hydrogen, and nitrous oxide its own volume of nitrogen). It follows, therefore, that the density of a gas is expressed by a number equal to one-half its molecular weight ($H = 1$).

It also follows that 22.4 litres of any gas weigh the number of grams expressed by the molecular weight of that gas ; for 11.2 litres of hydrogen weigh 1 gram, then 22.4 litres of hydrogen weigh 2 grams ; also 22.4 litres of another gas, whose molecular weight is x will weigh $2 \times x \times \frac{1}{2} = x$.

This result is constantly used in chemical calculations in translating weights into volumes and vice versa.

Example.

How many litres of nitrous oxide may be obtained by the decomposition of 30 grams of ammonium nitrate?

Solution,—

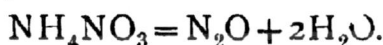

$$NH_4NO_3 = N_2O + 2H_2O.$$
80 parts give 44 parts by weight,

∴ 30 grams give $\frac{44}{80} \times 30 = \frac{33}{2}$ grams.

And since 22.4 litres weigh 44 grams, $\frac{33}{2}$ grams occupy $\frac{22.4}{10} \times \frac{1}{44} \times \frac{33}{2} = 8.4$ litres.

————

3.

It may be well to remind the student here of two physical laws that affect the volume of a fixed weight of a gas, and must, therefore, be taken into account in all calculations, except when the standard conditions of temperature and pressure exist. These laws are BOYLE'S and CHARLES'. The former relates to pressure. and tells us that, when temperature is constant, the volume of a quantity of gas confined in a closed vessel varies inversely as the pressure to which it is subjected. The latter relates to temperature, and according to it the volume of a quantity of gas increases $\frac{1}{273}$ part of its volume at 0°C. for every degree centigrade through which its temperature is raised. If a quantity of gas occupied 'a' vols. at pressure x, and if the pressure changed to 'y,' the volume would then be

$a \times \frac{x}{y}$; also if the temperature at first was t °C., then if this changed to p °C., the correction would be obtained by using the factors $\frac{273}{273+t}$ and $\frac{273+p}{273}$, the former to change to volume at 0°, the latter to change from volume at 0° to that at p°. The entire corrections for temperature and pressure would then be $a \times \dfrac{x}{y} \times \dfrac{273+p}{273+t}$.

_____

4.—Questions and Exercises.

Assume standard temperature and pressure, unless others are given.

1. How many grams of hydrogen will occupy 224 litres at the standard temperature and pressure?

2. Steam is passed through a tube containing red-hot iron filings, 18 litres of hydrogen pass out at the other end. What volume of steam was decomposed, and how much are the iron filings increased in weight?

3. How much sulphuric acid and zinc must be taken to form 112 litres of hydrogen at 7° C.?

4. In 285 grams of caustic potash how many grams of potassium? of hydrogen?

5. What weight of sodium must be taken to obtain 20 grains of hydrogen from a litre of water? If temperature were raised to 70° C. and pressure to 800 mm., what would the answer then be?

6. A reservoir of hydrogen gas holds 89·6 litres. What weight of water will be formed in burning the gas in air? What volume of air will be required for the combustion, assuming that oxygen forms 21% of the volume of air?

7. I want 220 grams of oxygen. If I obtain it from potassic chlorate, how much of it must I use? If from water, how much? If from mercuric oxide, how much? What volume at 15° C. and 200 mm. pressure would this gas occupy?

8. A gas bag is capable of containing 56 litres, how much potassic chlorate must be taken to procure enough oxygen to fill it at 35° C. and 750 mm.?

9. 25 litres of oxygen are exploded with 36 of hydrogen. What volume of gas (if any) remains? What volume of steam is produced? And what is its weight?

10. How much oxygen can be obtained from 435 grams of manganese dioxide by heating it to a red heat? (The reaction is $3MnO_2 = Mn_3O_4 + O_2$). What volume will it occupy at 30° C. and 780 mm.?

11. What volume will 80 grams of oxygen occupy at the standard temperature and pressure? At 62° and 790 mm.?

12. How much potassium will be required to decompose 110 grams of carbon dioxide? What weight of each of the products will be formed?

13. If 10 litres of carbon dioxide be passed over red-hot charcoal, what gas, and how many litres of it, will be formed at 30° C.? What weight of it?

14. 20 litres of carbonic oxide are burned in oxygen gas. What gas is produced, what volume at 40° C. and what weight of it?

15. How much carbon can be obtained from 264 grams of carbon dioxide? Would change of pressure vary the answer?

16. What volume of oxygen at 10° C. is required to burn 66 grams of carbon? How would the volume of the gas formed compare with that of the oxygen used?

17. In question 5, what volume of air at 740 mm. would be needed for the combustion of the hydrogen at 0° C.?

18. What volume do 110 grams of carbon dioxide occupy at 760 mm. pressure and 0° C.?

19. What volume do 140 grams of carbonic oxide occupy at standard temperature and pressure?

20. What weight of carbon dioxide can be obtained from 250 grams of pure limestone by treating with hydric chloride?

21. What weight of carbonate of lime and hydric chloride must be decomposed to produce 352 grams of carbon dioxide?

22. What volume will 98 grams of carbonic oxide occupy at 72, mm. pressure and 40° C.?

23. If 270 grams of oxalic acid be decomposed by sulphuric acid, find the volume of the gases produced at 750 m. pressure and 20° C.

CHAPTER XXVIII.

CARBON AND HYDROGEN.

1.—Hydrocarbons.

A large number of compounds of carbon and hydrogen are known under the general name of hydrocarbons. So numerous are these compounds, and those which carbon forms with oxygen, nitrogen, sulphur and phosphorus, that their mere names would fill a small volume. The study of the carbon compounds forms a distinct branch of chemistry under the name of organic chemistry. Formerly, this name included the study of those compounds which, it was supposed, were formed only by the agency of life; but it was soon found that there was no essential difference between chemical substances whether of animal, vegetable or mineral origin. The division of chemistry, therefore, into organic and inorganic, is a pure matter of convenience. The last-named division of the science treats of the composition and properties of air, earth and water, whereas organic chemistry may be said to be the chemistry of the carbon compounds.

Marsh gas is the first of a series of hydrocarbons known as the marsh gas series. Each member of it differs from the following one by CH_2. There is a difference of 30° between the boiling points of successive members. All are inflammable. There is also a regular increase or decrease of other physical properties. Such series are called homologous series. The general algebraic formula for the series is C_nH_{2n+2}.

2.—Methane.

Methane (Marsh Gas, Light Carburetted Hydrogen, "Fire-damp"), CH_4; molecular weight, 16; vapour density, 8.

EXPERIMENTS.

1. Take a hard glass test-tube or Florence flask and fit it with a cork and fine delivery tube (a copper retort used for preparation of oxygen is preferable as there is no danger of breaking it). Place in the test-tube 4 grams of acetate of sodium, $NaC_2H_3O_2$, 8 grams of sodium hydroxide, and 4 grams of finely-powdered quicklime, CaO. Heat. After collecting a beaker or two of the gas, light the jet and observe the colour of the flame.

Before lighting the gas, test it in the same way as hydrogen to see that it is not mixed with air.

The formula for this reaction is

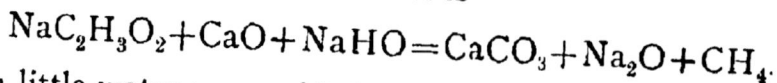

$$NaC_2H_3O_2 + CaO + NaHO = CaCO_3 + Na_2O + CH_4.$$

If a little water were added, so as to change the oxide of calcium into the hydrate, a second decomposition would have occurred, thus :

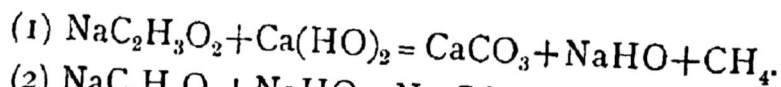

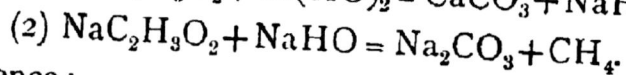

(1) $NaC_2H_3O_2 + Ca(HO)_2 = CaCO_3 + NaHO + CH_4.$

(2) $NaC_2H_3O_2 + NaHO = Na_2CO_3 + CH_4.$

hence :

(3) $2NaC_2H_3O_2 + Ca(HO)_2 = Na_2CO_3 + CaCO_3 + 2CH_4.$

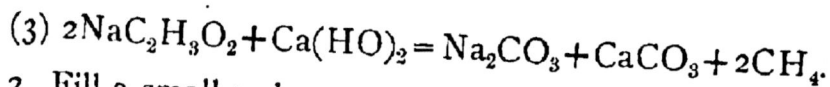

2. Fill a small soda water bottle with a mixture of one part of the gas and two parts of oxygen. Ignite the mixture. Express the reaction by an equation.

3. Take a stoppered bottle and fill it with a mixture of equal volumes of marsh gas and chlorine. Expose to sunlight for a day, then test the contents with blue litmus. Note any change in colour.

3.—Questions and Exercises.

1. Devise an experiment to ascertain whether marsh gas is acid or basic in reaction.

2. Devise simple experiments to prove that the gas contains carbon and hydrogen as constituent elements.

3. Prove that the gas is lighter than air. How would you distinguish the gas from air ?

4.—Notes.

Methane is generated in marshes by the decomposition of vegetable matter containing carbon and hydrogen. It is formed in coal mines also, and, on being mixed with air and ignited, causes fearful explosions, hence in miners' language it is "fire damp." To prevent these accidents Sir H. Davy invented his celebrated **Safety Lamp.**

5.—Olefiant Gas.

This is the old name of another gas that may be taken as a type of a second series of the hydrocarbons. The general formula of the homologues of this series is C_nH_{2n}.

Ethylene (Ethene. Olefiant gas. Heavy carburetted hydrogen), C_2H_4; molecular weight, 28; vapour density, 14.

EXPERIMENTS.

1. Into a Florence flask pour 50 or 60 c.c. of strong sulphuric acid and half that volume of alcohol. Insert a tightly-fitting cork and delivery tube. Place the flask on a retort stand and heat gently. After the air has all been expelled, collect two or three jars of the gas.

Alcohol has the formula C_2H_6O. The sulphuric acid acts here in the same way that it does on oxalic acid in the preparation of carbonic oxide, viz , by extracting the elements of water.

$$C_2H_6O + H_2SO_4 = C_2H_4 + H_2SO_4 + H_2O.$$

2. Ascertain whether the gas will burn or not. Has it any taste?

3. Devise simple experiments to prove that the gas contains hydrogen and carbon.

4. Find out whether the gas is heavier or lighter than air.

10

5. Remove a jar of the gas, let it drain well, then turn it mouth upward and place over it another jar of the same size filled with chlorine. After standing for some time, note whether the colour of the chlorine changes. Observe closely what forms at the bottom of the lower jar (" Dutch liquid.")

6. Ascertain whether the gas will explode when mixed with air or oxygen.

7. Is it soluble in water?

6.—Acetylene.

Acetylene, another hydrocarbon that has the formula C_2H_2, may become of great economic importance for illuminating purposes, because of a recently-discovered method by which it can be produced at small expense in large quantities. When calcium carbonate and powdered coal are heated in an electric furnace, calcium carbide, CaC_2, is formed. This, when immersed in water, readily yields acetylene, and the gas burns with great luminosity in the air, when ignited. The products of the reaction by which the acetylene is formed are calcic hydrate and acetylene, thus :—

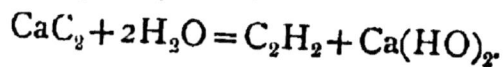

$$CaC_2 + 2H_2O = C_2H_2 + Ca(HO)_2.$$

CHAPTER XXIX.

COAL GAS AND FLAME.

1.—Coal Gas.

Coal gas is formed by the distillation of coal in large iron retorts. The process of manufacturing it may be illustrated by strongly heating some powdered soft coal in a common clay pipe. The mouth of the pipe should be closed with kneaded clay. The average composition of coal gas (for it is really a mixture of many gases) is about as follows :—

Hydrogen	45·
Marsh gas	35·
Carbonic oxide	7·
Olefiant gas	4·
Butylene	2·4
Hydric sulphide	0·3
Nitrogen	2·5
Carbon dioxide	3·8
Total	100· vols.

When the gas comes from the retort it contains a much larger quantity of hydric sulphide carbon dioxide and ammonia. It undergoes certain purifying processes, notably, a washing in a stream of cold water which causes the precipitation of tarry ingredients and the solution of a large portion of the ammonia. Any ingredient of coal gas which either does not burn with a luminous flame, or does not help to support the combustion of the other substances is objectionable, and should be got rid of, if possible. Hydric sulphide will burn readily, but one of the products of its combustion is a very undesirable substance to have mixed with the air of dwellings. The water in which the gas is washed yields, on proper treatment, our supply of two important substances, ammonia and coal tar. From the latter, are manufactured the beautiful aniline dyes so extensively used in recent years.

2.—Luminosity of Flame.

Now that we have learned something of carbon, hydrogen, oxygen, and a few of the compounds which they form, we are in a position to study somewhat more fully than we have hitherto done, the subject of combustion, with reference to the luminosity, or light giving properties of flames.

EXPERIMENTS.

1. Sprinkle into the flame of an alcohol lamp or Bunsen burner, some fine iron filings.

2. Rub together over the top of any non-luminous flame, two pieces of charcoal. Repeat, using two pieces of chalk.

3. Hold a piece of platinum wire or a piece of lime in the flame of hydrogen gas.

4. Observe closely the flame of an alcohol lamp, and if possible take it into a dark room to test its illuminating powers. Hold a cold plate horizontally in the flame for a minute; then blow out the flame and put into the lamp about one-half as much spirits of turpentine as there is of alcohol, quickly light the lamp and observe the

change that comes over the character of the flame ; again hold a cold plate in it. Repeat, but use a teaspoonful of benzine instead of the turpentine.

3.—Questions and Exercises.

1. From what source did the light emanate in all three experiments?

2. Mention one way of changing a non-luminous flame into a luminous one.

3. Explain the source of the black mark formed on a white plate by holding it horizontally across the flame of a candle, or of a coal oil lamp. What is the black substance?

4. How do you explain the facts observed in your experiments with oxygen, viz., that sulphur and phosphorus give more light when burned in oxygen than in air?

5. In experiment 4, sec. 2, turpentine is a hydrocarbon having the formula $C_{10}H_{16}$, and benzine has the formula C_6H_6, can you now account for the change in the flame and for the dark spot on the plate?

6. Close the holes at the base of a Bunsen burner, turn on the gas and light it. What kind of flame is there? Turn off the gas and invert a common funnel over the burner, as in Fig. 36, still leaving the holes at the base closed ; turn on the gas and after a few seconds light it at the end of the funnel stem. What sort of a flame is there now? Why?

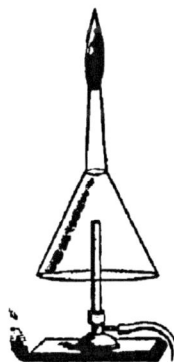

Fig. 36.

4.—Structure of Flame.

1. Spread out the wick of a candle or alcohol lamp, light it, and then thrust into the middle of the flame the phosphorus end of a friction match.

2. Float a small cork upon a little common alcohol or methylated spirits placed in the bottom of a small saucer. Place a few grains of gunpowder upon the cork, and then ignite the alcohol.

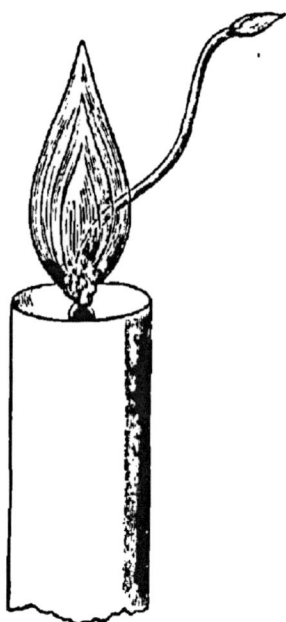

FIG. 37.

3. Bring a piece of wire gauze down horizontally upon the flame of a candle, of a coal oil lamp, or alcohol lamp.

4. Light a candle and observe its flame carefully. Note how many parts there are in it. Take a narrow bent glass tube, about four or five inches long, and thrust one end of it into the dark cone in the middle of the flame, as in Fig. 37. Try to light the vapours which rise through the tube. Repeat the experiment but use a Bunsen burner instead of the candle Try, both when the holes at the base are open and when they are closed. Why can you not get this result with a common coal oil lamp? Try a lamp that has a circular wick.

Explanation.—It is customary to speak of a flame as being made up of three parts; these are—1st, the central cone, consisting of gas that is not ignited; 2nd, the luminous mantle in which co'' going on; this is the chief light giving [ater mantle which is usually but slightly l inou nd n which combustion of the gaseous substance is completed. In the central cone the gas is still unburned. In the candle flame it is formed by the fatty constituents of the wa or tallow being drawn up through the wick from the little reservoir of melted matter surrounding it, and these are freed at the top of the wick in the form of vapour by the heat of the surrounding flame. As no oxygen is in contact with this gas it will not burn. A current of air is, however, being drawn into the vapour at the base of the flame around the wick, and the oxygen of this air causes the outer layer of the central cone to undergo constant combustion, with the result that the carbon particles in this mantle become incandescent. In the outer layer or mantle of the flame, air has become freely mixed with the vapour, and this vapour has been largely deprived of solid carbon particles while it was in the middle (luminous) mantle, so that it now burns with a nearly non-luminous flame. The middle and outside mantles correspond respectively to a Bunsen's flame with the holes at the base of the burner closed and then open. The central cone is called that of non-combustion, the next one, that of incomplete combustion, and the outer one that of completed combustion.

5.—Ignition.

The temperature at which a substance begins to burn is called its temperature of ignition, or its kindling point. Do all substances ignite at the same temperature?

EXPERIMENTS.

1. Pour a little carbon bisulphide into a large test-tube. Close with the thumb, and shake well, so that the vapour will fill the tube. Then warm a glass rod and place it in the vapour. If there be no result, heat the rod more strongly and again place it in the vapour.

2. Try to light coal gas with a rod similarly warmed; then with an iron rod nearly red hot; and lastly with an iron rod at a white heat.

6.—Questions and Exercises.

1. Why is it harder to light a coal fire than a wood one?

2. If you cool a burning substance, will it cease to burn? Investigate this point by making a small cone-shaped helix of copper wire and covering a candle flame with it. Heat the helix to redness and again place it over the flame.

3. Investigate the principle of the Davy lamp, used to prevent explosions in coal mines. The "fire damp" burns on the inside of the wire gauze which surrounds the flame. Why does not the gas outside take fire? Hold a piece of fine wire gauze two or three inches above a Bunsen's burner, turn on the gas, and after a few seconds ignite it on the upper side of the gauze.

4. Why does blowing on a flame "*put it out*"?

5. 5 grains of methane are burned in air. What would be the weight of the products of combustion? How could these products be collected for weighing? What weight of air would be required in order to complete the combustion? Change all weights into volumes, giving the answers in litres.

6. Try by experiment what changes a blowpipe makes in the flame of a candle, (1) as regards its size, and (2) as regards its heat?

7. In using a blowpipe, which is preferable to use for the blast, air exhaled from the lungs, or air that has been simply drawn into the mouth?

8. If a splinter of wood be placed across the flame of an alcohol lamp where does the wood begin to burn first? Test the accuracy of your conjecture by actual experiment.

9. What shaped mark will a candle flame make upon a piece of white letter-paper, when pressed for an instant horizontally upon the flame? Press the paper down almost to the wick, and remove quickly.

10. In the case of a candle flame, whence comes the gas that forms the flame?

11. Why should the outer mantle (of complete combustion) be more prominent in a candle flame than in that of a Bunsen burner?

12. Which is hotter, the luminous or the non-luminous flame of a Bunsen burner? Test by noting the time required to heat a piece of wire red hot, when held in about the same position in both flames.

13. What effect has a lamp chimney on the luminosity and temperature of a coal-oil lamp flame?

14. "Flame is incandescent gas." "Only gases burn with a flame." Examine these statements in the light of the experiments you have just made, or of observations which you have made on flames in coal or wood stoves.

15. If flame is incandescent gas, whence comes the gas that produces the flame when phosphorus burns in oxygen, sulphur in air or sodium on water?

16. A piece of paper dipped in turpentine, $C_{10}H_{16}$, when ignited in the air burns with a sooty smoke coming off from it. A piece of paper dipped in alcohol, C_2H_6O, when ignited, burns with an almost non-luminous flame and without smoke. Why the difference?

7.—Additional Exercises.

1. Examine the flame of a Bunsen burner, first, when the air holes are closed, then, when open. Note consequent changes in the temperature and luminosity of the flame. Pass in nitrogen or carbon dioxide through the air holes instead of air, and compare changes thus produced with those that took place in admitting air.

2. If in sec. 6, question 5, the gas burned had been olefiant gas instead of methane, what would then have been the answers to the questions?

3. Ten volumes of hydrogen, 10 volumes of carbonic oxide, 10 volumes of marsh gas, and 10 volumes of olefiant gas are each mixed with 25 volumes of oxygen and the mixtures burned. If the

products of combustion remain as gases, state what would be their volume at 100°C. and 750 mm. pressure.

4. A mixture of hydrogen and carbonic oxide, obtained by blowing jets of steam into white hot coals, is used as an illuminant, and is known technically as *water gas* (to distinguish it from coal gas obtained by the distillation of coal). Explain the chemical reactions, with equations, that go on in the preparation of this gas; also the chemical changes, and the value of each constituent for illuminating purposes.

5. Why is the burner of a gas jet made with an opening in the form of a slit instead of a round hole? and why is an argand burner made to allow air to pass up the middle of it?

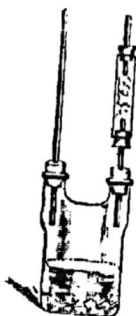

Fig. 38.

6. Use a two-necked Woulff's jar as a hydrogen generator, arrange it as shown in Fig. 38, putting a plug of cotton wool in the wide tube; after all the air is driven out set fire to the hydrogen escaping from both tubes. Remove the stopper from the large tube, pour two or three drops of benzine (C_6H_6) on the cotton, replace the stopper and again ignite the gas. How do you account for the change?

7. "Soft coal" or bituminous coal burns with a bright luminous flame, "hard coal" or anthracite glows, and burns away almost entirely without flame. How do you account for the difference?

8. A lamp flame turned too high will *smoke;* of what does this smoke consist? Whence does it come? Why is it formed only when the flame is turned too high? How do you account for the clouds of black smoke that come out of factory chimneys? If you are told that this smoke escapes most freely just after fresh coal has been put on the fire, would the statement confirm your explanation? Explain the "burning of smoke" in factories.

8.—Blowpipe Flame.

Three zones are observed when flame has a jet of air blown into it from the nozzle of a blowpipe. The inner mantle or zone of incomplete combustion, R, Fig. 39, is technically known as the *reducing flame*, because here the supply of oxygen is limited, hence the carbon has been oxidized only to carbonic oxide, and there is, therefore, a great tendency to take oxygen away from any

Fig. 39.

substance that will part with it. The outer mantle, O, is the *oxidizing* flame, because the supply of oxygen is plentiful, and the heating of a substance to a high degree in contact with oxygen of course promotes chemical union between the two, if that is possible.

References—Tilden, 64 ; R., 399 ; R. and S., 187.

CHAPTER XXX.

CHLORINE.

1.—The Halogens.

There are four elements—chlorine, bromine, iodine and fluorine—that are closely related to one another, and are known in chemistry as *halogens* (salt producers).

Chlorine is the most important of these. They all form acids that do not contain oxygen; these are sometimes called *haloid acids*, and the salts which they form, *haloid salts*; they are thus distinguished from salts and acids which contain oxygen.

2.—Experiments with Chlorine.

1. Into a test-tube put one part of manganese dioxide, two parts of salt, and three of sulphuric acid. Fit the test-tube with a cork and delivery tube. Heat gently. Cautiously smell the gas that comes off. Note its colour.

2. To prepare the gas on a larger scale, take a 4 oz. Florence flask and place in it about 20 grams of manganese dioxide and 100 c.c. of strong hydrochloric acid. Use fittings similar to those in Fig. 40. Apply a *very* gentle heat. The delivery tube should pass almost to the bottom of the jar. Fill several jars, taking care that little or none of the gas escapes into the room.

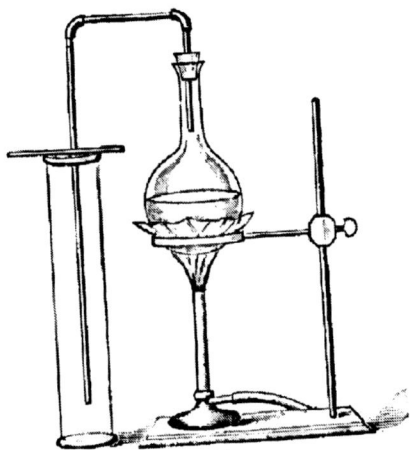
FIG. 40.

Place a wet glass cover over each jar. Afterwards pass the gas into a flask perfectly *full* of water; in about ten minutes place this flask aside for future use. Smell the water. The decompositions, which result in free chlorine being formed in the first of these experiments, may be represented by the following equations :—

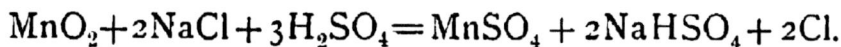

$$MnO_2 + 2NaCl + 3H_2SO_4 = MnSO_4 + 2NaHSO_4 + 2Cl.$$

This occurs in two steps thus :

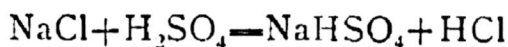

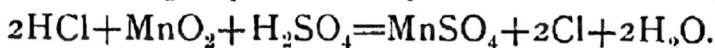

$$NaCl + H_2SO_4 = NaHSO_4 + HCl$$
$$2HCl + MnO_2 + H_2SO_4 = MnSO_4 + 2Cl + 2H_2O.$$

If these reactions go on together, there are being produced at the same time nascent oxygen, hydrogen and chlorine ; of these the oxygen and hydrogen unite and the chlorine remains free. The sum of these two reactions is indicated in the first equation.

The reaction that occurs in the second experiment may be represented as follows :—

$$MnO_2 + 4HCl = MnCl_2 + 2H_2O + 2Cl.$$

3. Take the flask full of chlorine water, prepared in the last experiment, and fit it with a cork and tube. The outer end of the tube must be drawn to a fine point. Insert the cork so that there is not a bubble of air left in the flask. Invert the flask as in Fig. 41, and expose to direct sunlight for a day. Then place the flask on the table, remove the cork, and quickly bring a glowing splinter to the mouth of the flask. Test the water in the flask with blue litmus solution. Taste it.

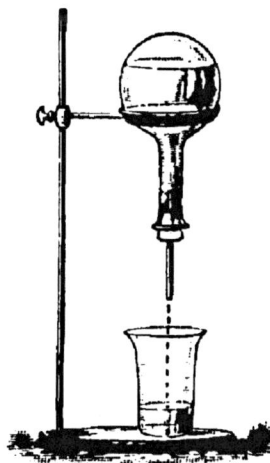

FIG. 41.

4. Lower very slowly a lighted taper into a jar of chlorine. At the same time suspend a piece of blue

litmus paper at the mouth of the jar. Smell the gas that is formed during the combustion.

5. Take a few pieces of the metal antimony and powder them; then place on a sheet of paper and shake the powder into a jar of chlorine. Try if arsenic acts similarly.

6. Fill a small jar with hydrogen, then bring its mouth below the mouth of another jar of chlorine. Keep the jars mouth to mouth, and invert them several times, so as to mix the gases thoroughly. Then separate the jars, carefully corking one, and applying a lighted match to the other. Wrap a towel around the jar which you have corked, so as to exclude the light, and carry it to where the sun is shining, either in a room or outside. Place it on the floor or on the ground and quickly unroll the towel so as to send the jar a short distance from you. Chlorine and hydrogen should never be mixed excepting in *dim* or *diffused light*.

7. Shake a tube full of the gas up with cold water to test its solubility.

8. Pass a current of chlorine, or pour some chlorine water, into solutions of logwood and of indigo.

9. Prepare chlorine as before, and cause it to bubble slowly through some strong sulphuric acid in order to dry it. Collect a jar of the dry gas and place in it pieces of dry calico of various colours. Close the jar tightly. Allow the calico to remain in the jar for about fifteen minutes. Then open the jar; quickly remove the calico, wet it in water, and return to the jar for fifteen minutes more.

3.—Bleaching by Chlorine.

Experiment 3, sec. 2, demonstrated the formation of oxygen by the action of chlorine on water; at the same time an acid was formed, and, as water and chlorine were the only substances present it is reasonable to assume that the chlorine decomposed the water molecules, joined with the hydrogen to form hydrochloric acid, and set the oxygen free. The latter gas, in the nascent state, is as we have already learned, a powerful oxidizing agent, and consequently unites with the colouring matters present and destroys them. Chlorine is, on this account, said to *bleach by oxidation.*

It is possible that in a few cases chlorine may combine directly with the hydrogen of the coloring matter, thus breaking up the compound. These cases are rare, for chlorine nearly always requires the presence of water for bleaching.

4.—Questions and Exercises.

1. Half fill a test-tube with hydrogen over water, then fill it up with chlorine, and let it stand over water for a few hours in diffused light. Test, with litmus paper, and with nitrate of silver solution, the water that passes into the tube.

2. Treat the refuse from preparing oxygen from manganese dioxide and chlorate of potash with sulphuric acid, and observe what gas is evolved. How do you account for this?

3. Take a piece of printed paper, write some words on it with lead pencil, and some with ink, then moisten the paper and drop it into a jar of chlorine. After half an hour examine it.

4. If chlorine bleaches by oxidation, and you wish to remove ink-stains from a handkerchief, why not plunge it into a jar of oxygen rather than one of chlorine?

5. Lower a piece of glowing charcoal gradually into a jar of chlorine; from the negative result of this experiment, explain the formation of the black smoke which escapes from the candle when burning in chlorine.

6. If the waste pipe of a kitchen sink were foul smelling, devise a method of deodorizing it.

5.—Additional Exercises.

1. Try if other chlorides may be substituted for common salt and hydric chloride in the preparation of chlorine, as in experiments 1 and 2, sec. 2.

2. Drop chlorine water into sodic hydrate solution until the mixture smells of chlorine after stirring, then evaporate to dryness. What remains? Why did a precipitate not appear?

3. Lower a piece of freshly cut phosphorus on a deflagrating spoon into a jar of chlorine.

4. The oxidizing power of chlorine may be shown in the following way :—

There are three oxides of lead, the protoxide, PbO, a buff or yellow powder, the red oxide, Pb_3O_4, a scarlet powder and the peroxide, PbO_2, a dark brown powder. They are all insoluble in water. If a little of the protoxide and of the red oxide be shaken up separately with water in test-tubes, and chlorine be then passed through the mixtures until the water is saturated, and the whole allowed to stand for some hours, the yellow and red powders will both be changed to brown, thus showing the change to the peroxide. This change may be hastened by using solution of potassic or sodic hydrate instead of water as the liquid with which the powder is mixed. Why?

5. Wet a piece of blotting paper with oil of turpentine, $C_{10}H_{16}$, and then place it in another jar of the gas. Use fresh and perfectly fluid turpentine.

6. Make a saturated solution of chlorine in water in a bottle, then immerse the bottle in a freezing mixture of ice and salt. Yellow

scale-like crystals should separate. These are supposed to be chlorine hydrate, $Cl + 5H_2O$. When warmed they decompose into chlorine and water.

---

6. -- Notes.

Chlorine: symbol Cl; mol. vol. 2 ; sp. gr. 2·47, (air = 1).

This element exists commonly as a gas, but may be obtained in the liquid form by enclosing crystals of chlorine hydrate in a strong tube and sealing off the part in which the yellow liquid chlorine condenses.

Chlorine is not valuable alone as a bleaching agent. In sanitary operations it is largely used as a **disinfectant** and **deodorant**. It here acts in the same way that it does in bleaching, viz., by indirect oxidation, or, possibly, at times by the direct union with the hydrogen in the noxious compound.

A **disinfectant** is a substance which arrests the spread of specific disease, by destroying the special agent that enters the body from without and causes the disease.

7.—Chlorine and the Alkaline Hydrates.

When chlorine is passed into a *cold* solution of potassic hydrate, a chemical action according to the following equation occurs :—

$$2KOH + Cl_2 = KCl + KClO + H_2O.$$

Potassic chloride, potassic hypochlorite and water are produced.

If the solution of the hydrate were *hot* a different combination would occur, thus ;—

$$6KHO + 3Cl_2 = 5KCl + KClO_3 + 3H_2O.$$

11

The reason for this change from the former result is that an alkaline hypochlorite in solution of an alkaline hydrate is easily decomposed by heat into the chloride and chlorate. The reaction expressed above really occurs in two steps, thus :—

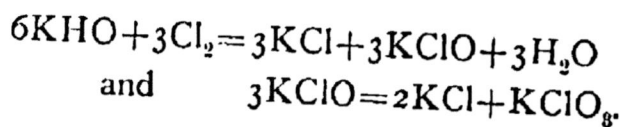

$$6KHO + 3Cl_2 = 3KCl + 3KClO + 3H_2O$$
$$\text{and} \qquad 3KClO = 2KCl + KClO_3.$$

This shows the effect of altered temperature in changing the products of a chemical experiment.

Chlorine, though very common in combination, does not occur free in nature. This is readily accounted for by its energetic chemical action with many elements, such as phosphorus, hydrogen, sodium, antimony and others.

The student should be able now to devise tests for chlorine and to give examples of its uses.

CHAPTER XXXI.

1.—Chlorine and Hydrogen.

Only one compound of chlorine and hydrogen is known, that is the haloid compound HCl, called hydric chloride or more commonly hydrochloric acid. A popular name for this substance is muriatic acid, from *muria, sea salt*, because the acid was prepared from the salts got by evaporating sea water.

2.—Hydrochloric Acid.

EXPERIMENTS.

It has been found that chlorine readily unites with hydrogen either when heated or exposed to light; also that chlorine decomposes water, forming a combination with the hydrogen and setting the oxygen free. In each case the combination was an acid.

1. Place some ammonic chloride in a medium-sized test-tube, and add a few drops of sulphuric acid. Bring a lighted match to the mouth of the test-tube; also a piece of blue litmus paper; and lastly, a glass rod dipped in ammonium hydroxide. Smell very cautiously.

2. Repeat this experiment, using a large test-tube or flask fitted with a cork or delivery tube, and substituting sodic chloride, NaCl, for the ammonic chloride. Use twice the weight of sulphuric acid that you do of salt, and apply heat very carefully. Collect some of the gas by passing the delivery tube to the bottom of an "empty" jar. Cover its mouth with a glass, plate. Having filled the jar, remove the plate cover and turn the jar mouth downward over some water coloured blue with litmus. Then shake slightly. Devise a means of finding out when the jar is full of the gas.

3. Fill a second jar with this gas, as before. Place two or three globules of sodium the size of a pea, in a deflagrating spoon, the handle of which passes through a cork that exactly fits the jar. Heat the sodium to ignition, and lower the spoon into the second jar of gas. After all action has ceased, withdraw the cork and quickly bring a lighted taper to the mouth of the jar. Dissolve the solid on the spoon and taste the solution.

4. Pass the gas into a solution of sodium hydrate until it is neutral to litmus, then evaporate. What compound have you? Write the equation.

5. Place a few pieces of zinc in a test-tube, and then pour upon them about 2 c.c. of hydrochloric acid. After all effervescence has ceased, remove the surplus zinc and evaporate the solution to dryness.

Commercial Acid.

A solution of this gas in water is what is usually sold by druggists under the name of hydrochloric or muriatic acid. How can the gas be obtained from such a solution? The commercial acid is prepared as a by-product in the manufacture of common "soda" by Leblanc's process. The solution of the acid is of varying strength, but about 33% by weight is the strongest solution that is permanent. Commercial acid contains about 20% of the gas.

3.—Aqua Regia.

A mixture of three volumes of hydrochloric acid and one volume of nitric acid is called aqua regia.

EXPERIMENTS.

1. Place a little piece of gold-leaf in chlorine water and let it stand for some time. Try what effect dry chlorine gas has on the gold-leaf.*

2. Place a few fragments of gold-leaf in a test-tube and pour upon them about 1 c.c. of hydrochloric acid.

---

*That which is sold as gold-leaf is often only a base alloy, so that these experiments may fail through impurity of the metal used. The gold-leaf should be tried first in strong nitric acid ; if it dissolves it is no good ; if, however, it is unaffected in the acid, it will be pure enough for the work here indicated.

Warm slightly. After a minute or two add a few drops of nitric acid.

3. Repeat the preceding experiment, using small scraps of platinum instead of gold.

Explanation.—The solvent action of *aqua regia* is due to chlorine which is freed by the action of the two acids on each other, thus :

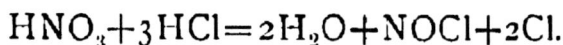

$$HNO_3 + 3HCl = 2H_2O + NOCl + 2Cl.$$

(NOCl is chloronitrous gas, or nitrosyl chloride). The chlorine readily attacks the gold or platinum to form the chloride, even when not in the nascent state.

4.—Composition of Hydrochloric Acid.

EXPERIMENTS.

1. Take a bent tube like that in Fig. 42. Partly fill the tube, as indicated, with hydrochloric acid, and insert in the ends the terminal wires of a battery. These terminals should be carbon. Bring a lighted match to that end of the tube connected with the zinc of the battery. Moisten a piece of coloured calico and place it over the other end of the tube. Colour the acid with litmus solution.

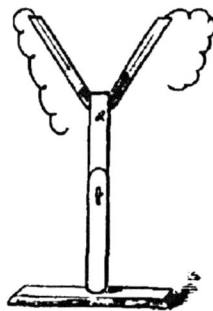

FIG. 42.

2. Pass about 25 c.c. of hydrochloric acid gas into a eudiometer over mercury, then introduce sodium amalgam until the gas ceases to contract in volume ; test the gas that remains.

5.—Questions and Exercises.

1. Will hydrochloric acid burn in air? Will it support the combustion of a candle?

2. An analysis of a piece of gold coin is required, how would you dissolve the metal?

3. In the experiments relating to the composition of hydrochloric acid, write the equations for all the reactions.

4. Suggest any reason why the terminal wires should be tipped with carbon, in the electrolysis of hydrochloric acid.

5. How is the "solvent" power of the acid increased?

6. Explain the effect of the acid gas on quicklime. To do this fill a tube with the gas over mercury, and then pass a piece of quicklime up under the mouth of the tube. Is this gas absorbed by charcoal? Find out by experiment.

7. How could you distinguish between this gas and chlorine?

———

The following simple method of determining the composition of hydrochloric acid gas is described in Reynold's Chemistry, Part II., page 69 :—

Open the stopcock, Fig. 43, and pass a current of hydrochloric acid gas through the U tube for some time, then quickly close the stopcock and pour mercury enough into the U tube to close the bend and half fill the open arm. Open the stopcock slightly and allow gas to escape until the mercury stands at nearly the same height in both arms. Mark the height of the mercury in the closed arm. Next drop into the open arm some sodium amalgam and fill to the top with mercury; close the open end with the thumb, and pass the gas backward

FIG. 43.

and forward a number of times through the mercury by tilting the tube. Finally hold the tube erect, raise the thumb and allow air to enter the open arm. Pour in or remove mercury until it is at the same height in both arms. The gas in the closed arm should now occupy half the volume that it did at first. Tilt the tube so that the mercury will press on the gas in the closed arm ; cautiously open the stopcock and hold the nozzle to a flame.

6.—Additional Exercises.

1. Try if any other chloride besides that of sodium can be used for the preparation of hydrochloric acid.

2. Would nitric acid answer instead of sulphuric? Base your answer on experiment.

3. Take 3 test-tubes ; half fill the first with a solution of silver nitrate, $Ag NO_3$; the second with a solution of mercuric nitrate, $Hg(NO_3)_2$; and the third with a solution of acetate of lead, $Pb(C_2H_3O_2)_2$. Into each tube pour a few drops of hydrochloric acid. Try to write the equations.

4. Place a little cupric oxide, CuO, in a test-tube and pour some hydrochloric acid upon it. When the oxide ceases to dissolve, filter, and evaporate the solution to dryness.

5. Try to form other chlorides by warming hydrochloric acid with metals, oxides or hydrates which you can find in the laboratory, and which you have not yet used.

6. Decompose some hydrochloric acid solution in a dark room by electricity. After this has gone on for some time so as to allow the liquid to become saturated with the escaping chlorine, collect some of the mixed gases and expose a measured volume to the action of solution of iodide of potash. When shrinkage has ceased, test the remaining gas.

7. What weight of common salt and sulphuric acid must be taken if it be required to liberate 146 grams of hydric chloride?

8. Calculate the amount of hydro-sodic sulphate that will be produced in generating 219 grams of hydric chloride from salt and sulphuric acid, at a moderate temperature.

9. Explain why we believe that hydrogen and chlorine are united in the proportions by weight of 1 to 35·5.

10. What volume will 73 grams of hydric chloride occupy at the standard temperature and pressure?

11. 10 grams of zinc are treated with dilute sulphuric acid in excess, the gas that comes off is burned in an atmosphere of chlorine, what volume would the product of the combustion occupy at 30° C and 750 mm. pressure?

7.—Notes on Hydrochloric Acid.

Hydrochloric acid gas or *hydric chloride: formula*, HCl; *mol. vol.*, 2; *mol. weight*, 73; *sp. gr.*, 1·27 (air=1); soluble in water to the extent of 480 times its own volume.

Commercial hydrochloric acid is one of the by-products in the preparation of soda, where sodium chloride is treated with sulphuric acid, and the escaping gas is intercepted and dissolved.

The white fumes observed when hydric chloride escapes into the air are due to the affinity of the acid gas for water, which causes a condensation of the aqueous vapour in the atmosphere.

The test for chlorides, including hydric chloride, is the white curdy precipitate they form with solution of silver nitrate.

1. Dissolve some common salt in half a test-tube full of pure water, and then add a few drops of nitrate of silver solution. Shake. Now pour half of the solution into a second test-tube; add a little nitric acid to the one test-tube and ammonium hydrate to the other. Boil the one to which you added nitric acid.

2. Repeat this experiment, using any soluble chloride in place of common salt.

CHAPTER XXXII.

1.—Some Compounds of Chlorine.

The compounds of chlorine are numerous and important, but only a few of them can be referred to here.

The chlorides of the alkalies can be prepared by either treating the metal with hydric chloride, by passing chlorine into the hydrate, or by bringing the metal into contact with chlorine. Most other metals form chlorides with hydrochloric acid.

The following paragraphs refer to the preparation and properties of a few of the important chlorine compounds.

2.—Bleaching Powder.

Bleaching powder, or chloride of lime, is an important article of commerce which is extensively used in bleaching the coarser kinds of cotton and linen goods. Its manufacture is illustrated in the following experiments.

EXPERIMENTS.

1. Cover the inside of a bell jar with slaked lime, and then pass chlorine into it for some time. The chemical changes which take place may be thus represented :

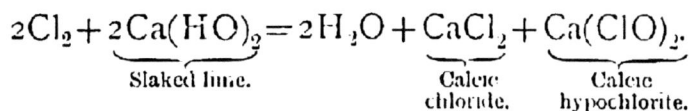

$$2Cl_2 + \underbrace{2Ca(HO)_2}_{\text{Slaked lime.}} = 2H_2O + \underbrace{CaCl_2}_{\substack{\text{Calcic} \\ \text{chloride.}}} + \underbrace{Ca(ClO)_2.}_{\substack{\text{Calcic} \\ \text{hypochlorite.}}}$$

It is this mixture of calcic chloride and calcic hypochlorite which forms the most important ingredients of what is popularly known as "bleaching powder."

2. Remove from the jar the product obtained in the preceding experiment. Place it in a soup-plate and add about 100 c. c. of water, stirring the mixture for five or ten minutes. Immerse in the solution thus prepared, a piece of printed calico. After a few minutes remove the calico and immerse it in a *very* dilute solution of sulphuric acid.

Bleaching powder, when acted on by sulphuric acid, yields chlorine slowly.

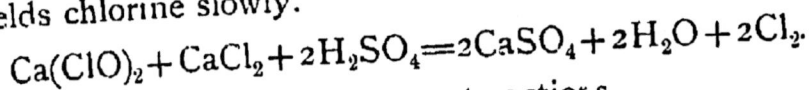

$$Ca(ClO)_2 + CaCl_2 + 2H_2SO_4 = 2CaSO_4 + 2H_2O + 2Cl_2.$$

This is the result of three separate actions.

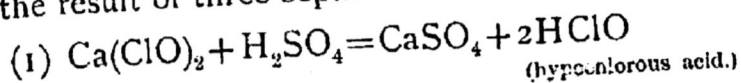

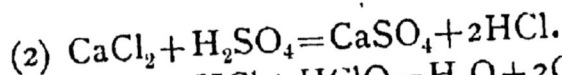

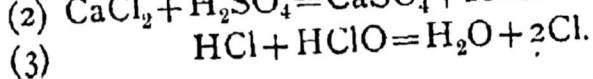

(1) $Ca(ClO)_2 + H_2SO_4 = CaSO_4 + 2HClO$
(hypochlorous acid.)

(2) $CaCl_2 + H_2SO_4 = CaSO_4 + 2HCl.$
(3) $HCl + HClO = H_2O + 2Cl.$

3.--Potassic Chlorate.

EXPERIMENTS.

1. Boil a strong solution of caustic potash in a test-tube and pass into it a current of chlorine for half an hour. Evaporate the solution to a small quantity and then allow it to cool slowly. Both potassic chloride KCl, and potassic chlorate $KClO_3$, will be formed in the solution. The latter being the least soluble crystallizes out *first*. The liquid that remains contains the potassic chloride in solution. Pour off this liquid. To purify the crystals re-dissolve them in a little hot water and allow them to reform. (Compare Chap. XXX, sec. 7.)

All the oxygen compounds of chlorine are unstable, and most of them are explosive, breaking up into chlorine and oxygen.

2. Put a crystal of chlorate of potash about the size of a pea into a test-tube, then drop in a little sulphuric acid and heat gently. While pouring in the acid, and while heating, keep the tube carefully pointed away from yourself and other persons near you.

The rather violent decomposition that goes on is expressed by the following equation :

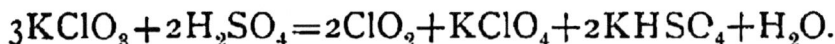

$$3KClO_3 + 2H_2SO_4 = 2ClO_2 + KClO_4 + 2KHSO_4 + H_2O.$$

This is the sum of the following reactions :

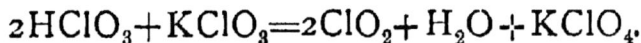

$$2KClO_3 + 2H_2SO_4 = 2KHSO_4 + 2HClO_3 \text{ (chloric acid)}.$$
$$2HClO_3 + KClO_3 = 2ClO_2 + H_2O + KClO_4.$$

The sulphuric acid and chlorate give rise to chloric acid, which immediately breaks up into chloric peroxide, water and oxygen, the latter uniting with a molecule of the chlorate to oxidize it to perchlorate.

3. In a conical vessel, such a as graduate, place a few crystals of chlorate of potash, on these lay two or three bits of freshly cut phosphorus, cover the whole with water to a depth of a couple of inches ; then, by means of a pipette, introduce a few drops of strong sulphuric acid among the lumps of chlorate. Compare this experiment with the preceding one and explain the result.

All chlorates yield oxygen readily. The following experiments go to prove the truth of this statement.

4. Powder a few of the crystals of chlorate of potash with a little charcoal and heat the mixture on a piece of mica.

5. Powder some more of the salt with dry sugar. Place

the mixture on a tin plate or piece of cardboard, and add a drop or two of sulphuric acid with a pipette.

6. Powder separately, and dry on a warm plate, some sulphur and chlorate of potash. Rub a *little* of the mixture on an iron plate with a pestle or hammer. This is dangerous, so only *small* quantities of the mixture should be made and used.

7. Dissolve a crystal of a chlorate in water; add a little indigo solution, and then a few drops of sulphuric acid. Explain the cause of the change of colour.

Tests for a chlorate.—Experiments 2 and 4 give tests sufficient to distinguish chlorates from other compounds.

4.—Oxides.

Oxygen forms with chlorine three well known oxides and two hypothetical ones.

FORMULA.	NAME.	CORRESPONDING ACID.
$Cl_2O.$	Hypochlorous anhydride.	HClO Hypochlorous acid
$Cl_2O_3.$	Chlorous anhydride.	$HClO_2$ Chlorous acid.
$Cl_2O_4,(ClO_2.)$	Chloric peroxide.	No corresponding acid.
$Cl_2O_5.$	Not eliminated.	$HClO_3$ Chloric acid.
$Cl_2O_7.$	Not eliminated.	$HClO_4$ Perchloric acid.

Just as sodium nitrate $NaNO_3$ yields nitric acid when treated with sulphuric acid; and sodic chloride NaCl yields hydrochloric acid; so potassium chlorate $KClO_3$

yields chloric acid $HClO_3$; and potassium hypochlorite yields hypochlorous acid $HClO$. Thus :

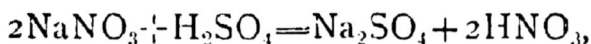

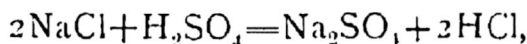

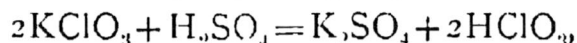

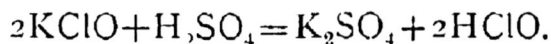

$$2NaNO_3 + H_2SO_4 = Na_2SO_4 + 2HNO_3,$$
$$2NaCl + H_2SO_4 = Na_2SO_4 + 2HCl,$$
$$2KClO_3 + H_2SO_4 = K_2SO_4 + 2HClO_3,$$
$$2KClO + H_2SO_4 = K_2SO_4 + 2HClO.$$

As chloric and hypochlorous acids, however, break up with dangerous explosions as soon as formed, the student is warned not to attempt to prepare them in this way.

5.—Questions and Exercises.

1. How can the chlorate of potash be converted into the chloride?

2. What physical state do the compounds formed in an explosion usually assume?

3. How much chlorine by weight and volume can be obtained from 1460 grams of hydric chloride?

4. How much chlorine can be liberated from 585 grams of common salt? What volume will it occupy at 60° F.?

5. What volume will 284 grams of chlorine occupy at 80° F?

6. What quantities of manganic sulphate, hydro-sodic sulphate, water, and chlorine, will be formed by the decompositions of 351 grams of common salt, with manganese dioxide and sulphuric acid?

7. If 142 grams of chlorine gas be passed into steam at a red heat, what substances will be formed, and what weight of each?

8. What weight of hydric chloride will 261 grams of manganese dioxide require for its decomposition?

9. Why should chlorate of potash decompose quietly when heated alone, but violently when heated with sulphuric acid?

10. Write the formulæ for sodium chlorite, magnesium chlorate, barium perchlorate, calcium chlorite, potassium hyposulphite.

11. Mention any advantage that results from the use of bleaching powder as a disinfectant in a room, rather than chlorine prepared as for experimental work.

12. Powder some chlorate of potash. Heat a little of it on a piece of mica having previously placed two or three small lumps of charcoal on the powder. Compare this with experiment 4, sec. 3. Account for the different results.

6.—Additional Exercises.

1. Make a solution of asafœtida by dissolving some of the substance in a little alcohol in a small beaker. Now add a few drops of sulphuric acid to a solution of bleaching powder, and then try what effect this solution will have on the solution of asafœtida. Does the oduor change?

2. Would any other acid added to bleaching powder produce the same effect that sulphuric acid does when added to it?

3. Had nitric acid been used instead of sulphuric in sec. 3, experiment 2, what would have been the result?

4. Try the effect of chlorine water on any bad smelling solution which you can secure, ammonium sulphide, for example.

5. Determine by experiment if other alkaline hydrates such as those of sodium and potassium will yield the analogues of bleaching powder. Write the equations in full for the reactions. Will the substances obtained bleach dyed goods? In these experiments keep the solutions *cool*.

6. What would be the result of passing a current of chlorine into lime water?

CHAPTER XXXIII.

1.—Sulphur.

EXPERIMENTS.

1. Place some sulphur on a metal spoon and hold it in a flame until ignited, then withdraw it. Notice the colour of the flame and the smell of the oxide that comes off. Do this by wafting the fumes toward the face with the open hand.

2. Place 15 or 20 grams of sulphur in a large test-tube and heat slowly over a lamp flame until the sulphur boils. As the heating goes on, note changes in the appearance of the substance. When it begins to boil, pour it into a vessel of cold water. When it has cooled, remove and examine. Burn a little of it as in the last experiment. Compare the colour of the flame and the odour of the vapour with those noticed before. Keep in a dry place for a few days, and then examine again.

3. Try if yellow sulphur is soluble in water, alcohol, chloroform, ether, spirits of turpentine, or carbon bi-sulphide.

4. Powder some iron pyrites, FeS_2, and place in a *hard* glass test-tube. Hold the test-tube nearly horizontally in the lamp flame and heat the lower end strongly for some time. Test the residue with a magnet. Observe what collects in the cool part of the test-tube.

2.—Questions and Exercises.

1. What physical property of sulphur is illustrated in the fourth experiment?

2. The residue from the iron pyrites has the composition Fe_2S_3. Write the equation expressing the reaction that took place.

3. Prepare some sulphur crystals by melting 40 or 50 grams of flowers of sulphur in a porcelain or earthenware dish, and then allowing it to cool slowly. When a thin crust has formed on the surface punch a couple of holes in it with a glass rod, pour out the liquid sulphur from the interior, and after the dish has cooled, carefully remove the surface crust.

4. Try to prepare some more crystals by dissolving sulphur in carbon disulphide and allowing the solution to evaporate.

5. Try whether plastic sulphur is soluble, as in experiment 3, sec. 1.

6. Describe in detail the changes which you noticed when sulphur was heated in a tube to boiling.

7. Fuse a little sulphur with some sodium carbonate; lay the fused mass on a piece of clean silver, and let a drop of water fall on it. *This is a test for free sulphur.*

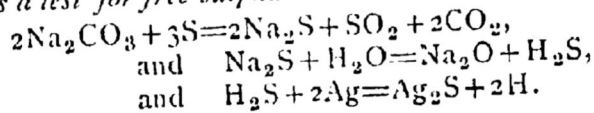

$$2Na_2CO_3 + 3S = 2Na_2S + SO_2 + 2CO_2,$$
$$\text{and} \quad Na_2S + H_2O = Na_2O + H_2S,$$
$$\text{and} \quad H_2S + 2Ag = Ag_2S + 2H.$$

3.—Additional Exercises.

1. Bend a piece of hard glass tubing as shown in Fig. 44. Place in it at A some iron pyrites and heat strongly in a flame, holding the longer arm of the tube at about 45° with the vertical. Smell the gas that comes off. How do you account for the result being different from that obtained in experiment 4, sec. 1?

Fig. 44.

Repeat the experiment, using galena, or lead sulphide, instead of pyrites.

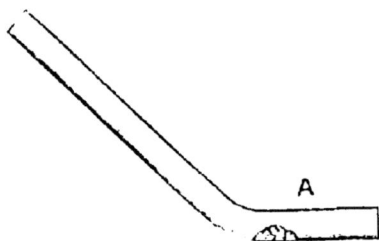

2. Boil some sulphur in a tube, and when the vapour is coming off freely lower into it separately a bit of sodium, a little coil of *fine* copper wire, and some fine iron filings. Then drop some hydrochloric acid on some fresh copper and iron filings, smell the gas that comes off. Treat the coil and filings that were in the **sulphur in a similar way.**

Explanation.—When iron is roasted with sulphur, the sulphide FeS is obtained. This, when acted on by hydrochloric acid, HCl, is decomposed, ferrous chloride, $FeCl_2$, and sulphuretted hydrogen, H_2S, being the result. The latter was the foul smelling gas that escaped.

———

4.—Abnormal Vapour Density of Sulphur.

Read Chapter XXVII.

The following is a tabulated statement of the molecular weights and densities of a few of the gases we have already become acquainted with :—

	Mol. Formula.	Mol. Weight.	Mol. Volume.	Vapour Density.
Hydrogen	H_2	2	2	1
Oxygen	O_2	32	2	16
Nitrogen............	N_2	28	2	14
Aqueous Vapour.....	H_2O	18	2	9
Nitrous oxide	N_2O	44	2	22
Nitric oxide........	NO	30	2	15
Ammonia	NH_3	17	2	8·5
Carbon dioxide	CO_2	44	2	22
Carbon monoxide	CO	28	2	14
Marsh gas	CH_4	16	2	8

From the examples given above it will be seen that in the column headed "Vapour Density" the numbers ex-

12

IMAGE EVALUATION
TEST TARGET (MT-3)

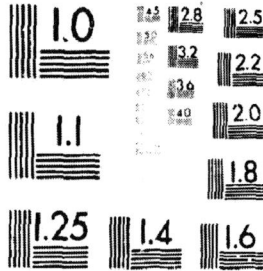

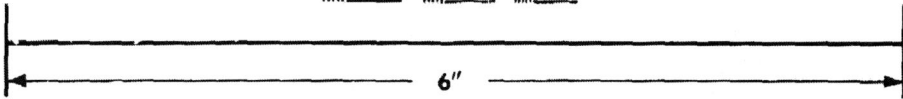

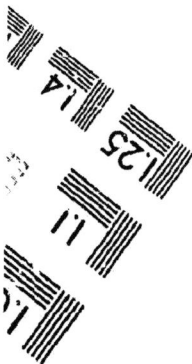

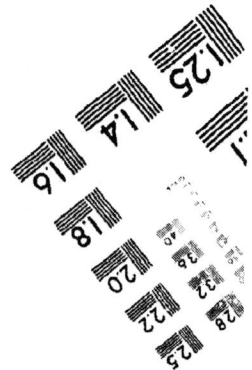

1.0

1.1

1.25   1.4   1.6

← 6″ →

Photographic
Sciences
Corporation

23 WEST MAIN STREET
WEBSTER, N.Y. 14580
(716) 872-4503

press the ratio between the molecular weight and the molecular volume of any gas. From Avogadro's Law we know that equal volumes of gases under like conditions contain equal numbers of molecules, hence any unusual vapour density must be due to an unusual number of atoms in the molecule rather than to any departure from the number of molecules in a unit volume of the gas showing the irregularity.

In the case of sulphur, it is found that near its boiling point (485°) the vapour density is 96, while at 850° this density is 32, in round numbers. When the vapour density is 96 the molecular weight must be 192, but at the higher temperature mentioned the molecular weight will be 64. Chemical analysis leads to the belief that sulphur has an atomic weight of 32. From this it is clear that, at about 500°, the molecule of sulphur consists of 6 atoms ; but at 850° and above that to 1200°, the molecule has in it only 2 atoms. A change of temperature, therefore, modifies the molecular structure of the substance, as is indicated by the change in the vapour density.

The vapour density of sulphur is treated in R. & S., p. 292, Vol. I.; Rem., pp. 89, 192 ; Wurtz, pp. 69-71 ; Tilden, p. 127-128 ; Rem. Th. Ch., 44.

5.—Notes on Sulphur.

Symbol, S ; atomic weight, 32 ; specific weight in the form of crystals, 2·05 (water = 1).

Sulphur, known also as brimstone, is found native in many volcanic regions; it occurs also in the ores of some of the common metals. Iron pyrites FeS_2, galena

PbS, cinnabar HgS, gypsum $CaSO_4 + 2H_2O$, and heavy spar $BaSO_4$, all contain sulphur. It is also found, as sulphuretted hydrogen, H_2S, dissolved in the waters of some springs, and in many substances of organic origin, such as albumen and coal.

6.—Allotropic Modifications.

Sulphur is known in three different forms; of these, two are modifications of the shape in which sulphur crystalizes; the third one, known as *plastic* sulphur, is prepared as described in experiment 2, sec. I, and is used for making moulds of coins, etc.

Common yellow sulphur, known as flowers of sulphur, or when run into cylindrical moulds, roll sulphur, may be taken as the first allotropic form. The crystalline structure can be studied with a magnifying glass. The second crystalline form is prepared as in experiment 3, sec. 2.

CHAPTER XXXIV.

Oxides of Sulphur.

There are two oxides of sulphur known—the dioxide SO_2 and the trioxide SO_3. Of these only the former will be treated of here, because the latter is difficult of preparation and comparatively of little importance.

1.—Sulphur Dioxide.

EXPERIMENTS.

1. In a flask, fitted with a cork and delivery tube, heat some copper clippings and sulphuric acid.

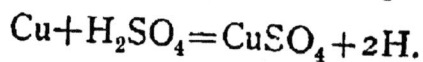

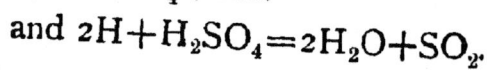

$$Cu + H_2SO_4 = CuSO_4 + 2H.$$
$$\text{and } 2H + H_2SO_4 = 2H_2O + SO_2.$$

These equations are usually written thus:—

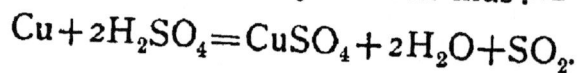

$$Cu + 2H_2SO_4 = CuSO_4 + 2H_2O + SO_2.$$

2. Collect a couple of bell jars full of the gas, test for solubility, acidity and inflammability.

3. Hang a red rose or other high-coloured flower in the second jar. If any change takes place in the flower, remove it and place in pure air.

4. An easy method for the preparation of sulphur dioxide is to treat some *sodium hyposulphite* $Na_2S_2O_3$ (which is chemically sodium thiosulphate) with sulphuric acid.

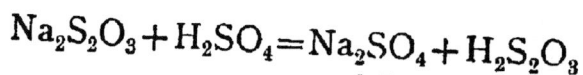

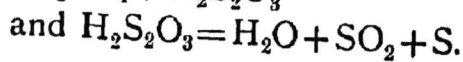

$$Na_2S_2O_3 + H_2SO_4 = Na_2SO_4 + H_2S_2O_3$$
$$\text{and } H_2S_2O_3 = H_2O + SO_2 + S.$$

Try this method.

5. Pass a current of the gas into solutions of logwood, indigo and permanganate of potash.

2.—Questions and Exercises.

1. Put some sulphur on a plate, set fire to it and turn an empty bell jar over it. After combustion has ceased compare the gas as regards solubility, odour and acidity with that obtained from copper and sulphuric acid.

2. Zinc and cold dilute sulphuric acid yield free hydrogen. Try if the same result follows if the acid be strong and hot. Smell the escaping gas, collect a test-tube full of it and try if it is all, or in part, hydrogen. Account for the results you obtain.

3.—Additional Exercises.

1. Pass some sulphur dioxide gas through a wash bottle, then into a solution of barium nitrate, add hydrochloric acid.

2. Pass some of the gas into water until the solution is distinctly acid, let this stand in an open vessel for a day, then test with barium nitrate and hydrochloric acid.

3. Heat together sulphur and sulphuric acid.

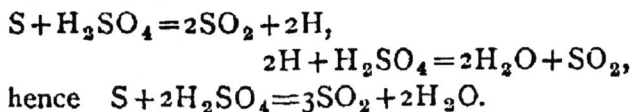

$$S + H_2SO_4 = 2SO_2 + 2H,$$
$$2H + H_2SO_4 = 2H_2O + SO_2,$$
hence $S + 2H_2SO_4 = 3SO_2 + 2H_2O.$

4. Heat together charcoal and sulphuric acid.

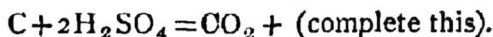

$$C + 2H_2SO_4 = CO_2 + \text{ (complete this)}.$$

5. Heat together manganese dioxide and sulphur.

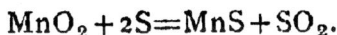

$$MnO_2 + 2S = MnS + SO_2.$$

6. Prepare some thin starch paste, add to it a little solution of potassic iodide, then drop into it a little chlorine water. After it has become blue make a thin solution of it in water in a test-tube, pass a current of sulphur dioxide through this.

7. Try if any sulphite which you can obtain will yield sulphur dioxide when treated with any strong acid.

4.—Notes on Sulphur Dioxide.

Symbol, SO_2; molecular weight, 64; vapour density, ($H=1$) 32.

Sulphur dioxide, on account of its strong affinity for oxygen, is a powerful reducing agent. It is used extensively both as a bleaching agent and as a disinfectant.

The power of sulphur dioxide to act in this way is supposed to be due to its affinity for oxygen. According to this theory the dioxide unites with the oxygen of the water which is used to moisten the article to be bleached; the hydrogen of the water then combines with the coloring matter and forms colourless compounds.

Tests (1) Odour.

      (2) See ex. 1, 2 and 6, sec. 3.

This gas is the anhydride of sulphurous acid, H_2SO_3.

CHAPTER XXXV.

Acids of Sulphur.

Sulphur, in union with hydrogen and oxygen, forms two well known acids, **sulphurous** and **sulphuric**. The following exercises will illustrate their preparation and some of their chief properties.

1.—Sulphurous Acid.

EXPERIMENTS.

1. Pass some sulphur dioxide gas slowly into water in a bottle. After some time test the water with litmus.

2. Divide the solution made in the previous experiment into two parts, with one of these fill a small bottle, cork it tightly and set it away for a couple of days. Pour a few drops of the other part into a test-tube, add

a little solution of barium nitrate (there should be no precipitate), then a drop or two of silver nitrate solution; set the remainder of this part away in an open beaker beside the bottle just mentioned. At the end of two or three days test each part of the liquid again. (Barium nitrate alone gives a white precipitate with sulphuric acid, but in the case of sulphurous acid this precipitate does not appear until silver nitrate is added.)

2.—Sulphuric Acid.

EXPERIMENTS.

1. Invert a jar of sulphur dioxide gas over a small beaker containing a little strong nitric acid.

2. Pour a little water into a large flask, then pass into it simultaneously brown fumes from a heated metallic nitrate and sulphur dioxide gas, also allow air free access into the flask. After about ten minutes, remove the connections, shake the water well with the gas in the flask, then test the liquid with barium nitrate.

Explanation.—Sulphur dioxide in presence of water or steam will readily reduce either nitrogen trioxide or peroxide to nitric oxide, and thus become itself oxidized to sulphuric acid.

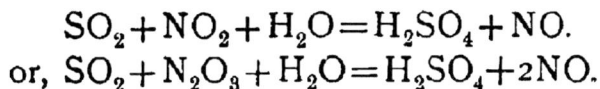

$$SO_2 + NO_2 + H_2O = H_2SO_4 + NO.$$
$$\text{or, } SO_2 + N_2O_3 + H_2O = H_2SO_4 + 2NO.$$

In either case the nitric oxide in presence of air at once changes back to the trioxide and is ready to yield up oxygen again; thus, this gas serves simply as a medium for transferring oxygen from the air to the sulphurous acid.

3.—Questions and Exercises.

1. Is barium sulphate soluble in nitric acid, sulphuric acid or ammonia? Is lead sulphate soluble in these liquids?

2. Sulphuric acid is prepared in quantity by leading into a lead-lined chamber the gases formed :—

(*a*) By roasting in air iron pyrites,

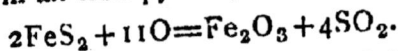

$$2FeS_2 + 11O = Fe_2O_3 + 4SO_2.$$

(*b*) By heating together sodic nitrate and sulphuric acid,

$$NaNO_3 + H_2SO_4 =$$

Steam is also passed into the chamber. The reaction may be represented as follows :—

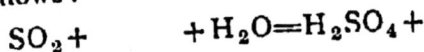

$$SO_2 + \qquad + H_2O = H_2SO_4 +$$

Complete the equations.

Why use lead as a lining for the chamber in preference to iron or zinc? Would you suspect that lead sulphate would be an impurity of the commercial acid?

3. Measure out accurately about 20 c.c. of strong sulphuric acid and an equal portion of water, then pour the acid in a thin stream into the water. What volume is there of the mixture? If change of volume and change of temperature indicate chemical action, how should this result be classed?

4. Given some sulphur, nitric acid and other necessaries, how would you proceed to prepare sulphuric acid?

5. A bottle containing sulphurous acid should be kept quite full. Why?

————

4.—Hydrogen and Sulphur.

Sulphur and hydrogen form one compound that is of very general application in chemical operations, and is an agent extensively applied in the separation of some of the more commonly occurring elements. This is *hydrogen sulphide, sulphuretted hydrogen* or *hydrosulphuric acid*, H_2S.

EXPERIMENTS.

1. On some iron sulphide (prepared by roasting a mixture of iron filings and about two-thirds as much sulphur, by weight, in a closed crucible) pour some dilute sulphuric acid. $FeS + H_2SO_4 = $ what?

2. Try if the gas given off is soluble in water; if you have reason to believe that it is, find whether the supposed solution is acid, alkaline or neutral.

3. Try whether the gas given off will burn. In case that it does, hold a cold, dry beaker inverted over the flame. Fasten on a piece of glass rod a strip of moist litmus paper, blue at one end, red at the other, and raise it into the beaker. What is being formed in the beaker?

4. Dip some pieces of soft white paper in a solution of acetate of lead, hold one of these in a current of hydrogen sulphide, dip another into a solution of the gas.

5. Let a drop of solution of the gas fall on a bright silver coin.

6. Make a bottle half full of strong solution of the gas, cork it tightly and set it away for a month. How do you account for the gray powder? Smell the liquid. Test it with the acetate of lead paper.

7. Pass a current of chlorine into a solution of hydrogen sulphide. $2Cl + H_2S = $ what?

5.—Questions and Exercises.

1. What is your opinion regarding the stability of hydrogen sulphide as a chemical compound? Quote as many proofs as you have seen in support of that opinion.

2. Hydrogen sulphide is one of the constituents of illuminating gas before it is purified. It is exceedingly objectionable, although readily combustible. Why?

3. Hydrogen will reduce heated copper oxide to metallic copper; sulphur will burn freely to form the dioxide. What should be the effect of hydrogen sulphide on such a substance (oxide of copper) when heated?

———

6.—Additional Exercises.

1. Drop a lump of white sugar into some strong sulphuric acid in an evaporating dish; let it stand for 24 hours, then dilute largely with water, filter, wash with water, dry and examine carefully. Try if a little of the black substance will burn on mica. Heat some of it in a combustion tube and lead the gas into lime water.

2. Repeat the preceding experiment, but instead of sugar use sawdust or wood shavings.

3. Try if any other sulphide such as that of copper (prepared in a way similar to that of iron) or lead, (galena) will yield sulphuretted hydrogen. Is it necessary that sulphuric acid should be used?

4. Repeat experiment 3, sec. 4, but use a bell jar fitted with a stopper instead of the beaker. When the jar is filled with the acid gas, set it, mouth downward, on a plate that has a little water on it, then extinguish the burning gas and turn the current of sulphuretted hydrogen into the bell jar.

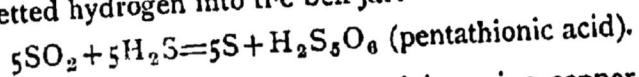

$$5SO_2 + 5H_2S = 5S + H_2S_5O_6 \text{ (pentathionic acid)}.$$

5. Make solutions of any salts of lead, iron, zinc, copper, mercury, barium, antimony, potassium. sodium, magnesium. Pass sulphuretted hydrogen into a part of each (if more convenient, a strong solution of the gas may be prepared and some of this poured into a solution of each salt). If no precipitate is obtained add hydrochloric acid to a part of the solution until it is distinctly acid, then use the sulphuretted hydrogen again. If no precipitate still, add ammonia to each solution until it is alkaline, then try again with the gas.

6. Ammonium sulphide $(NH_4)_2S$ is prepared by passing hydrogen sulphide through a solution of ammonia; do it. Will this give

precipitates with any of the solutions used in the preceding experiment?

7. Pass a current of steam through a combustion tube in which some sulphur is heated. What comes off? Substitute hydrogen for steam. What now is formed?

8. Given a constant current of sulphide of hydrogen, some nitric acid and some pieces of iron wire, how could you illustrate the preparation of sulphuric acid?

9. Compare oxide of hydrogen and sulphide of hydrogen as to (1) the compounds from which they are prepared, (2) their syntheses, (3) their acidity, (4) their stability, (5) their chemical action with metallic salts, (6) their molecular constitution.

7.—Notes on Hydrogen Sulphide.

Symbol, H_2S ; mol. wt., 34 ; mol. vol., 2 ; sp. gr. 1·19, (air=1).

It is a poisonous gas, soluble in water in proportion of 3 to 1 by volume, occurs frequently in natural water, particularly of springs, and is formed largely in the decay of organic matters.

In analysis of chemical compounds sulphuretted hydrogen is a valuable group test for the metals, that is, by its aid they are divided into three classes :

(1) Those whose sulphides are precipitated from acid solutions (copper group or hydrogen sulphide group). The common metals of this group are copper, lead, mercury, silver, bismuth, antimony, arsenic, tin.

(2) Those whose sulphides are precipitated from alkaline solutions only, such as iron, nickel, cobalt, zinc.

(3) Metals whose sulphides are not precipitated from any solution; the alkalies are examples.

Tests for the gas are (1) its odour, (2) its effect on acetate of lead solution, or paper dipped in it, and (3) its effect on silver.

CHAPTER XXXVI.

Calculation of Formulæ.

In chapter XXV the calculation of empirical formulæ of compounds was discussed when the percentage composition was known. At that time one important fact for the accurate determination of the molecular formulæ had not been learned, viz.: that the vapour density of a substance is one-half its molecular weight. Vapour density is always taken with hydrogen as the unit. A couple of examples will be solved to show the application of this principle :—

1. A compound, on analysis yielded

hydrogen, 2·25 %
carbon,   26·65 %
oxygen,   71·2 %

Its vapour density is 45, find its formula.

$$2·25 \div 1 = 2·25$$
$$26·65 \div 12 = 2·25$$
$$71·2 \div 16 = 4·45$$

Neglecting what are probably errors of experiment, the

elements are present in proportion of 1, 1 and 2. The formula may, therefore, be either HCO_2, $H_2C_2O_4$, $H_3C_3O_6$, etc. The vapour density is 45, therefore the molecular weight is 90. Now, starting with the lowest empirical formula, we find that it gives a molecular weight of 45, just half that required. We must, therefore, double the number of atoms, and write the formula $H_2C_2O_4$ (oxalic acid).

2. A hydrocarbon, when analyzed, gave hydrogen, 7·7 %; carbon, 92·2 %; its vapour density is 39, determine its formula.

$$7·7 \div 1 = 7·7$$
$$92·2 \div 12 = 7·7$$

Therefore the proportions of hydrogen and carbon are as 1 to 1. Hence the formula is H_nC_n, where n is any integer. The molecular weight of the substance is $39 \times 2 = 78$.

The molecular weight of HC is 13.

$78 \div 13 = 6$, hence formula is C_6H_6 (benzine).

CHAPTER XXXVII.

Impurities in Air and Water.

It is desirable that every one should be able to determine, approximately at least, the degree of purity of the two substances which are most necessary for our existence, in order that hurtful impurities may be removed or rejected. These substances are the air we breathe and the water we use for drinking and for domestic purposes.

1.—Air.

The atmosphere is a mixture of a number of gaseous substances some of which are quite variable in quantity; but it is generally considered that a mixture of oxygen and nitrogen in the proportion of 21% by volume of the former to 79% of the latter shall be taken as pure air. The chief gases mixed with these are aqueous vapour, carbon dioxide, and traces of ammonia It would seem from recent investigations that are not yet finished (Feb'y, 1895) that there is a third constant constituent of the atmosphere, Argon, and possibly a fourth; but at present it may be passed over with a mere mention.

Two experiments may be repeated for determining the carbon dioxide and vapour of water in the atmosphere. The first is 3, Chap. XXVII, sec. 4. This experiment may be varied by driving a measured volume of air backward and forward a number of times through a weighed quantity of strong solution of caustic potash, then weighing the solution.

When it is necessary to test the purity of air for breathing in such places as school rooms, dwellings and lecture halls, the quantity of carbonic acid gas per thousand volumes is generally taken as the test of purity. This is not an absolute test, for there may be and indeed generally are other objectionable and deleterious products of respiration present, but as they always accompany the carbon dioxide the latter is used as the basis of the measurement. There are about 4 parts of carbon dioxide to 10,000 of air in the atmosphere. When the proportion rises above 10 in 10,000, on account of impurities due to respiration, the air becomes very objectionable for breathing.

2.—Water.

Pure water is both scarce and difficult to prepare. Probably the purest natural water is that which has recently fallen as rain, away from the neighbourhood of towns and factories. It is then much in the condition of the water prepared by distillation. Water which has lain in contact with the earth for some time is sure to become impregnated with mineral salts and decaying matters of various kinds.

Natural waters are classified as *hard* and *soft*.

Water that contains magnesium, and calcium salts, and that curdles soap, is said to be *hard;* water that does not contain these salts is *soft.* Hardness is usually considered as being of two kinds, viz., *temporary* and *permanent.* The former is due to the presence of calcic and magnesic carbonate, the latter to the presence of salts of calcium and magnesium other than the carbonates, such as the sulphates and nitrates.

Water that is temporarily hard may be softened by boiling, because the carbonates are held in solution by the carbonic acid dissolved in the water or the bicarbonate is itself soluble. Boiling expels the carbon dioxide or decomposes the bicarbonate and the carbonate is precipitated.

Water that is permanently hard may be frequently softened by the use of washing soda—neutral sodium carbonate, Na_2CO_3. (Compare Chap. XXVI.)

Complete the two following equations. When complete they represent the reaction of washing soda on two kinds of hard water.

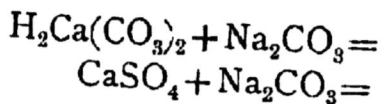

$$H_2Ca(CO_3)_2 + Na_2CO_3 =$$
$$CaSO_4 + Na_2CO_3 =$$

Water suitable for drinking is described as **potable**. That which comes from springs generally contains mineral salts, such as the carbonate of calcium or other substances through which the water has trickled, in solution. These salts are not necessarily objectionable— indeed the flat taste of rain water and of distilled water is due to the absence of them, and to the lack of aeration.

Organic matters, however, when held in solution, frequently render water dangerous to use. One test for such impurities depends on the decolorization of permanganate of potash by them.

1. Place the water to be tested in a flask, and add to it, first, a few drops of sulphuric acid, and then enough of a solution of permanganate of potash to give to the whole a purple tint. Set to one side for three or four hours in a warm place, and if the solution loses its colour, organic impurities are present. Water that will thus decolorize permanganate of potash is in all probability unfit for drinking. If it is necessary to use such water, it should first be boiled for at least half an hour.

2. Rub a chalk crayon on the hands until they become covered with the dust, then try to make a lather with a little water and soap.

CHAPTER XXXVIII.

1.—Molecules of Elements Usually Consist of More Than One Atom.

The only perfectly reliable means which we possess for ascertaining the molecular weight of a compound is the determination of its *vapour density*.

It follows from Avogadro's Law that the weights of individual molecules of different gases is proportional to the weights of equal volumes of these gases. All we have to do then, in order to find the relative weights of molecules of different gases, is to weigh equal volumes of them under like conditions of temperature and pressure, and the numbers thus obtained will represent the relative weights of a single molecule of each gas. Manifestly, any gas might be taken as a standard with which to compare the weights of all other gaseous substances; but, for many reasons, it has been found preferable to take hydrogen as the unit of comparison.

The following facts have been established by actual weighing :—

1 litre of oxygen weighs   .   .   .   .   1.429 gram.
1   "   nitrogen   "   .   .   .   . 1.2553   "
1   "   chlorine   "   .   .   .   .   3.167   "
1   "   hydrochloric acid gas weighs 1.6283   "
1   "   hydrogen weighs 0896   "

(The weight of hydrogen is obtained by calculation from the two preceding data, because it is exceedingly difficult to weigh a litre of hydrogen accurately, on account of its lightness.)

Now, using hydrogen as the standard of comparison, it follows from the above data that oxygen is nearly

13

sixteen times heavier than hydrogen; nitrogen, nearly fourteen times heavier; and chlorine, 35.34 times heavier. Hence, these figures represent the number of times that a molecule of each of these elements is heavier than a molecule of hydrogen. It follows, further, that if we know the actual number of atoms composing each of these molecules, we should be able to calculate their atomic weights. If there are the same number of atoms (say two) in each molecule of these elements, the above figures will also represent their atomic weights, one atom of hydrogen being taken as the standard. Of course, no one knows how many atoms there are in the molecule of any of the elements, but the following considerations will help the pupil to understand the conventional ideas on this subject.

2.—The Molecule of Oxygen Consists of at Least Two Atoms.

Two volumes of hydrogen and one volume of oxygen unite to form two volumes of steam.

From this it follows that two molecules of hydrogen and one molecule of oxygen unite to form two molecules of water. In one molecule of water there must be one molecule of hydrogen and half a molecule of oxygen, therefore this half molecule must consist of at least one atom.

3.—The Hydrogen Molecule Consists of Two Atoms at Least.

We h see.1, in Chap. XXXI, that two volumes of hydrocl...ric acid gas may be broken up into one volume

of hydrogen and one volume of chlorine. One volume
of the acid may, therefore, be divided into half a volume
of hydrogen and half a volume of chlorine. Then one
molecule of the acid consists of half a molecule of each
constituent, and this half molecule must be at least one
atom ; hence, the molecule of hydrogen has in it two
atoms at least.

Since this substance is the standard for vapour density
comparison, we have to rely on other considerations for
the proof that the molecule consists of only two atoms.
Some of these are :—In compounds of hydrogen with
monad elements the combinations and decompositions
take place each at one stage; never is part of the hydrogen freed from the other element, and then by changed
or intensified treatment, the other part liberated. On
the other hand, when hydrogen unites with a diad
element, half of it may frequently be displaced at once,
and the other half at another time. Thus :—

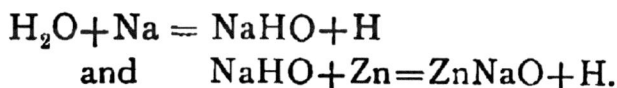

$$H_2O + Na = NaHO + H$$
$$\text{and} \quad NaHO + Zn = ZnNaO + H.$$

With monads such displacements are manifestly
impossible.

When decomposition of such compounds (hydrogen
with monad elements) occurs, the hydrogen always
occupies one half the space of the original gas ; hence,
from two molecules of the compound, one molecule of
hydrogen is set free. The same conclusion is arrived
at from the consideration that in equal volumes of
hydrogen and hydrochloric acid gas, the weight of
hydrogen in the latter, when freed, is just half that of
the former ; hence, in equal volumes of hydrogen and

hydrochloric acid, the number of molecules being equal, the number of hydrogen molecules formed from the latter gas equals half that existing in the former. Since in chemical decompositions the quantity of hydrogen freed from combination with monad elements is the unit of volume, of which that liberated from other combinations is always an integral multiple, it is reasonable to conclude that we have here the smallest subdivisions of the hydrogen molecule which have existence, *i.e.,* half molecules or atoms.

4.—Nitrogen Molecules.

When nitrous oxide was decomposed by burning potassium (see Chap. XX), a volume of nitrogen equal to that of the original gas remained. When nitric oxide was similarly treated the nitrogen remaining was half that of the gas taken. Now it will be evident that equal volumes of the two oxides contain equal numbers of molecules, and that every molecule of the nitrous oxide contains nitrogen sufficient to form one molecule of that gas, while in the case of the nitric oxide each molecule contains only half a molecule of nitrogen, hence the molecule of nitrogen is divisible into two equal parts, hence, contains at least two atoms.

5.—Chlorine Molecules.

We have learned that the hydrogen molecule has in it two atoms; also one volume of hydrogen unites with one volume of chlorine to form two volumes of hydrochloric acid. The analysis of the latter shows that it is composed of equal parts, by volume, of hydrogen and chlorine; then, since one volume of the gas is made up of half a volume of hydrogen and half a volume of chlorine, it follows that one molecule of it is composed of half a molecule of hydrogen and half a molecule of chlorine; hence, the chlorine molecule is divisible into two equal parts, or at least into two atoms.

6.—Other Elements.

Starting with the compounds marsh gas and sulphur dioxide, the conclusion follows that sulphur and carbon molecules are also divisible into at least two equal parts or atoms.

The student must not understand, however, that this is a proof that there are only two atoms in the molecules of these substances. While that is probably the case with most elements, it has already been shown that for sulphur there are six atoms in the molecule at certain temperatures. Phosphorus and arsenic have each a four-atom molecule, while ozone has three, and mercury one.

In the case of compounds, it follows directly from the atomic theory that the molecule must consist of a group of atoms,—one at least from each constituent.

CHAPTER XXXIX.

The following questions have been selected, partly from recent Pass Matriculation and Junior Leaving examination papers, partly from other sources. They are here simply as an indication of the standard of efficiency which scholars have been required to reach in the past few years.

I. SERIES.

1. On what grounds do you consider Hydrogen and Oxygen to be chemical elements, and water to be a compound of these two elements?

2. Describe as fully as you can, the phenomena of a solution of a salt in water.

3. A test-tube is known to contain distilled water, or a solution of one of the following: Ammonia Gas, Potassium Hydrate, Potassium Chloride, Nitric Acid. How would you determine most simply which the test-tube contains?

4. Explain by means of equations, how each of the following substances bleaches:

(a) Chlorine in the air.
(b) Chlorine in a solution of water.
(c) Sulphur Dioxide Gas.

5. Sulphur Dioxide: how prepared? how converted into Sulphur Trioxide? How would you prove that Sulphur Dioxide contains its own volume of Oxygen?

6. Calculate the weight of the product or products in each of the following cases:

(a) One gram of Carbon Monoxide burned in Oxygen.
(b) One gram of Ammonia Gas burned in Oxygen.
(c) One gram of Sodium burned in Chlorine.

7. How is Ammonia Gas prepared from Ammonium Chloride? Calculate how much heavier it is than Hydrogen and how much lighter than Nitrogen? How could you show that it contains both Nitrogen and Hydrogen?

8. Describe experiments showing how you would distinguish

(a) Carbon Monoxide from Hydrogen.

(b) Carbon Dioxide from Nitrogen.

(c) Marsh Gas from Hydrogen. ⁻

II. SERIES.

1. (a) Describe experiments to show that one c.c. of Hydrogen Gas and one c.c. of Chlorine Gas are found in two c.c. of Hydro-chloric Acid Gas, and one c.c. of Oxygen Gas and two c.c. of Hydrogen Gas in two c.c. of Water Gas.

(b) Draw the inference from the above experiments that the ratio of the weight of two c.c. of each of these compound gases to the weight of one c.c. of Hydrogen is twice the Specific Gravity of the Compound Gases compared to Hydrogen.

2. Discuss the question as to the distinction between a combustible substance and a supporter of combustion. Illustrate by equations the chemical reactions which occur in the combustion of

(a) Hydrogen in Chlorine.

(b) Oxygen in Marsh Gas.

(c) Carbon Monoxide in Oxygen.

(d) Sodium in Hydrochloric Acid Gas.

(e) Hydrogen Sulphide in Oxygen.

3. Explain the meaning assigned by Chemists to the following terms : (a) Oxidizing Agents, (b) Reducing Agents ; write equations showing instances of oxidation, (c) by Oxygen Gas, (d) by Chlorine Water, (e) by Nitric Acid ; of reduction (f) by heat, (g) by Charcoal, (h) by Nascent Hydrogen.

4. Describe the physical changes and illustrate by equations the chemical changes which occur when each of the following substances is heated in a test-tube, (a) Ammonium Nitrate, (b) Potassium Nitrate, (c) Lead Nitrate, (d) Calcium Carbonate, (e) Ammonium Chloride.

5. Name and give the formulæ of the substances formed by the action of hot Concentrated Sulphuric Acid upon each of the following bodies: (a) Copper, (b) Charcoal, (c) Potassium Chlorate, (d) Ammonium Nitrate, (e) Ammonium Chloride, (f) Calcium Carbonate.

6. Explain the chemical and physical reactions which occur in the following experiments—give equations in each case :

(a) A small piece of Sodium is thrown upon Water.
(b) A small piece of Potassium is thrown upon Water
(c) Chlorine Gas is mixed with Hydrogen Sulphide.
(d) Charcoal is heated with Sulphur Vapour.
(e) Nitrogen Trioxide is mixed with Sulphur Dioxide.

7. Describe experiments showing how you would distinguish

(a) Oxygen from Nitrous Oxide.
(b) Nitrous Oxide from Nitric Oxide.

8. Write equations explaining the reactions when Chlorine is passed into

(i.) Dry Ammonia,
(ii.) Solution of Potassium Iodide,
(iii.) Hot solution of Potassium Hydrate.

9. In what respects do the properties of Hydric Nitrate differ from Potassium Nitrate and Potassium Hydrate?

III. SERIES.

1. (a) State the effect of Carbon Bisulphide upon each of the forms of Sulphur.

(b) What is the action of Hydrogen Sulphide upon Sulphur Dioxide?

2. How would you prove the presence of

(a) Hydrogen and Sulphur in Hydrogen Sulphide,
(b) Carbon in Carbon Dioxide,
(c) Nitrogen in Ammonia?

3. Give one illustration in each case showing the relations of Electricity, Heat, and Light, as a cause, and an effect of chemical action.

4. Describe, giving equations, what occurs in each of the following experiments :

(*a*) Copper wire and strong Sulphuric Acid are heated together in a flask and the gaseous product passed into a solution of caustic potash.

(*b*) Hydrochloric Acid is added to pulverized Barium Dioxide and the resulting mixture boiled.

5. Each of five bottles contains one of the following gases :

Hydrochloric Acid Gas, Sulphur Dioxide, Carbon Monoxide, Nitric Oxide, Carbon Dioxide.

Describe how you would most easily determine the gas in each bottle.

6. (*a*) State briefly one of the theories usually held regarding solution.

(*b*) Describe two methods of determining the percentage composition of sand and ammonium carbonate present in a mixture of 100 grams of these substances.

7. When houses are heated with hot water passing through iron pipes from an iron furnace, a substance which plumbers call " air " collects in the uppermost parts of the pipes. This "air" burns with a pale-blue flame and forms a mist on any cold solid held over it. Name the gas and explain its formation by means of an equation. Give also the product of its combustion.

8. When a coal fire gets low, then throwing much coal on it, or greatly increasing the draft will frequently put the fire entirely out. Why? Describe an experiment which illustrates the correctness of your explanation.

9. Heat in a flask fitted with cork and delivery tube a mixture of dry powdered quicklime and ammonic chloride. Pass the gas that comes off into pure water until no more will dissolve. Neutralize this water with pure nitric acid and then evaporate to dryness. Heat on a piece of mica the solid that remains. Name the final products and explain the whole series of changes.

10. Explain the meaning of the following equations :—H_3PO_4 —$H_2O = HPO_3$. How is the operation carried out in the laboratory? What is the *test* for the last substance or its salts?

11. (*a*) If you are in doubt as to whether a solid is soluble in water or not, describe an experiment which you would perform to decide the point.

(*b*) How would you separate a finely powdered mixture of sand, sugar and iron, so as to preserve the first two substances?

12. (*a*) Describe fully how you would prepare some metallic copper from copper sulphate, and metallic silver from silver nitrate.

(*b*) How would you prove the presence of the acids in these salts?

13. Explain, using equations, the reactions that occur when

(*a*) Carbon dioxide is passed over red hot charcoal,
(*b*) Dry hydrogen is passed over red hot copper oxide.

14. Compare the action of hot sulphuric acid on copper with that of strong nitric acid on copper. Give equations.

IV. SERIES.

1. Nitric acid may be prepared by heating sodic nitrate with sulphuric acid. When the other substance formed is acid sulphate of sodium, find in what proportions the substances must be taken that none of either may be left. What is acid sulphate of sodium? When is such a salt possible? Write the equation for the other reaction possible between the substances.

2. A current of ammonia gas is passed into water for some time, then nitric acid is added until the solution is neutral; afterwards the liquid is evaporated and the residue heated in a test-tube, what will be the final products? Give equations.

3. Four volumes of methane are mixed with six volumes of oxygen and the mixture exploded. Find the volume of the gas in the vessel and state its composition (1) at a temperature of 120°, (2) after the products of combustion have stood in a room at 20° c. for some time.

4. Make a strong solution of ammonic chloride in a beaker, test the solution with litmus. Then hang a piece of litmus paper just above the liquid, but not touching it, place another piece in the solution, and boil the contents of the beaker for half an hour. State what will occur, and explain the chemical action.

5. Some chlorine, carbon dioxide and sulphur dioxide are mixed in a jar, this jar is then placed mouth downwards over a dish containing a solution of sodium hydrate in excess. Explain, with equations, the chemical changes that will have taken place at the end of a couple of days.

6. In a flask, A, is heated a mixture of sal ammoniac and potassic hydrate, both in solution. The resultant gas is led into another flask, B, which contains a little water. At the same time some manganese dioxide and sulphuric acid are added to a third flask, C, in which has been placed some of the liquid residue from the preparation of carbon dioxide, by the action of hydrochloric acid on an excess of calcic carbonate. The flask, C, is also heated, and the gas formed led into B. Explain the series of chemical changes.

7. 10 grams of sulphuric acid is diluted and added to an excess of sulphide of iron ; the gas that comes off is burned in air. How many grams of air will be required to complete the combustion? Find the volume of each product of the combustion at 120° C. and 750 mm. pressure.

8. You are given copper clippings, iron wire, sulphur, sulphuric acid, saltpetre, water, all necessary apparatus. Mention at least a dozen compounds that could be formed from them. State how you would proceed in each case.

9. Some sodium is thrown upon water, then hydrochloric acid is added until the solution is neutral to litmus. The liquid is evaporated to dryness and divided into two parts ; both are heated with sulphuric acid, but to one manganese dioxide has been added as well. The resultant gases are led into separate solutions of sodium carbonate. After a few hours, argentic nitrate is added to both solutions. Explain the series of chemical actions, with equations.

V. SERIES.

1. You are given (a) 5 white powders and are told that they are sodium carbonate, sodium nitrate, potassium chloride, zinc sulphate, potassium oxide.

(b) 5 bottles of liquid and are told that they contain solutions of chlorine, carbon dioxide, ammonia, hydrochloric acid and hydrogen sulphide.

(c) 8 jars of transparent gas containing separately, hydrogen, nitrous oxide, nitric oxide, carbon monoxide, carbon dioxide, oxygen, nitrogen and air. Describe how you would test each group in order to determine the substances.

2. A piece of sodium was completely converted into chloride by uniting with 200 c. c. of Cl. at the standard temperature and pressure. What was the weight of the sodium?

3. Name the chief oxidizing agents with which you have experimented, and explain the theory of the action of each.

4. What experiments have you made that illustrate the direct replacement of hydrogen by steam?

5. How many grams of nitric acid containing 67·2 % of pure HNO_3, will neutralize 54·4 grams of ammonia containing 36 % of NH_3?

6. Chlorine was formerly regarded as a compound of hydrochloric acid gas with oxygen. Describe experiments, proving that this was an incorrect view.

7. State in each case the simplest mode of determining when a receiver is full, in the preparation of ammonia, chlorine, carbon dioxide, and sulphur dioxide. How would you transfer each of these gases from one receiver to another?

8. With some water containing CO_2 in solution, is shaken up a mixture of pure sand and NaCl.

(1) How would you separate these four substances?

(2) How would you prove that you had separated them?

9. Matter is said to be composed of the elements. Give several illustrations of the facts which lead to this theory, and explain why you consider a mixture of equal volumes of hydrogen and chlorine gases to be a "mixture" before explosion, and to be replaced by a "compound" after explosion.

VI. SERIES.

1. A solid substance contains both a carbonate and an easily dissolved sulphide. How would you prove the presence of these two bodies?

2. Carbonate of ammonia and nitric acid are given you. How would you prepare nitrous oxide from these? Give equation. Draw apparatus used.

3. You have given to you some sulphur, water, and nitric acid. Describe how you would make sulphuric acid from these materials.

4. How could carbon monoxide be shown to contain half its volume of oxygen?

5. Each of two flasks contains some hydrochloric acid, into one is dropped some iron filings, into the other some manganese dioxide, then both are heated. The gases that come off are led simultaneously through a hot tube, thence into a solution of potassic carbonate. Trace the chemical changes throughout.

6. Nitrogen may be prepared by using copper clippings, nitric acid and air. It may also be got from ammonium nitrate. Explain the process in each case.

7. If carbon were the element of reference for atomic weights, find what numbers would express the atomic weights of magnesium, chlorine, sulphur, arsenic, iron, mercury. Find also the molecular weights of hydroxyl, carbonic anhydride, nitric acid and ozone.

8. The formula for alcohol is C_2H_6O. If a lamp burns 10 grams of alcohol, find the weight of water produced by the combustion, also how many litres of air would be necessary to furnish the oxygen required.

9. Some copper wire is gently warmed with nitric acid, and the gas that comes off is collected over water. A jar full of this gas is placed, mouth downward, over calcic hydrate solution, then oxygen is very slowly forced into it. What chemical changes go on?

10. Show, from experiment, that (a) change of temperature may affect the chemical results when the substances act on each other, (b) that the masses of the two substances may affect the result, (c) that the degree of concentration of one or both constituents may alter the substance formed.

11. The following mixtures of gases are given you, and you are required to separate them, but to preserve the first of each group as a gas, (a) nitrogen and oxygen, (b) nitrogen and hydrogen, (c) carbon monoxide and carbon dioxide, (d) hydrogen and sulphur dioxide, (e) oxygen and hydrochloric acid, (f) nitrous oxide and nitric oxide. How would you proceed in each case?

APPENDIX.

The following books should form a portion of the reference library of every high school. The publishers' names are appended, but the latest editions should be asked for by those who will purchase them. The letters after the names are the contractions used in the references in this book :—

Roscoe and Schorlemmer's Treatise on Chemistry (R. & S.), Vols. I. and II. (2 parts). Macmillan & Co.

Remsen's Inorganic Chemistry (R.). Advanced series. H. Holt & Co.

Reynold's Experimental Chemistry. Parts I. to IV. Longmans, Green & Co.

Muir and Slater's Elementary Chemistry. Cambridge University Press.

Remsen's Theoretical Chemistry (Rem. Th. Ch.). Henry C. Lea.

Wurtz Atomic Theory (Wurtz). International Scientific Series, Vol. XXX. D. Appleton & Co.

Richter's Inorganic Chemistry. Blakiston, Son & Co.

Chemical Theory for Beginners, by Dobbin and Walker (D. & W.). Macmillan & Co.

Ramsay's Proofs of Chemical Theory. Macmillan & Co.

Tilden's Introduction to Chemical Philosophy (Tilden). Longmans, Green & Co.

Bloxam's Chemistry. Henry C. Lea.

The following is the work in chemistry prescribed for the years 1896-97-98. An experimental course defined as follows :—Properties of Hydrogen, Chlorine, Oxygen, Sulphur, Nitrogen, Carbon, and their more important compounds. Nomenclature. Laws of Combination of the Elements. The Atomic Theory and Molecular Theory.

Teachers who are not supplied with gas holders will find a contrivance similar to that of the accompanying figure a great convenience.

It consists of a large bottle (a glazed earthenware jar will answer well) fitted with a perforated rubber stopper, and a pail with a stopcock at the bottom. The bottle may be filled with gas just as any other vessel would be, then the stopper may be inserted and the clips closed. In this way the gas may be stored until wanted. When the gas is required it is only necessary to connect the apparatus as in the figure, open the clips and allow the water to flow—the rate may be regulated by the stopcock. When it is necessary to draw a current of gas through any apparatus, the tube B may be disconnected from the stopcock, the positions of the bottle and pail interchanged, the bottle filled with water, and a piece of tubing connected with B long enough to reach below the bottom of the bottle. As the water is siphoned out at B, air or other gas will flow in at A. A more convenient arrangement still is to have the tube B about 4 or 5 feet long, then to cause a flow one way or the other it is simply necessary to interchange the positions of pail and bottle.

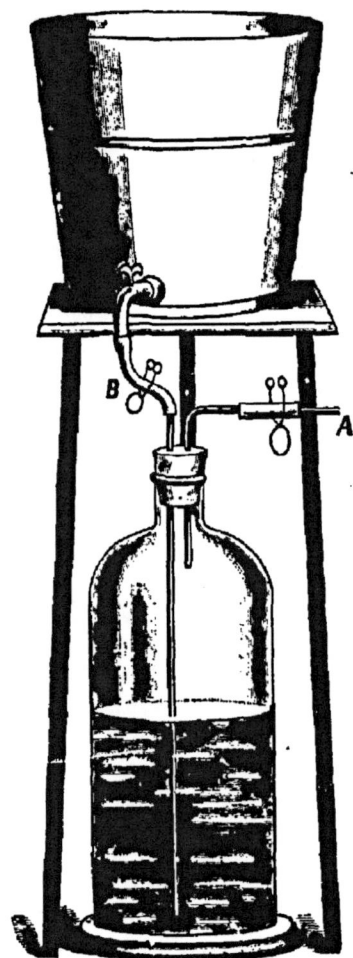

FIG. 45.

INDEX.

INDEX.

LaVergne, TN USA
28 June 2010
187671LV00004B/17/P